FROM THORNS TO BLOSSOMS

Mitzi Asai Loftus

with David Loftus

From Thorns to Blossoms

A Japanese American
Family in War and Peace

Oregon State University Press
Corvallis

Oregon State University Press in Corvallis, Oregon, is located within the traditional homelands of the Mary's River or Ampinefu Band of Kalapuya. Following the Willamette Valley Treaty of 1855, Kalapuya people were forcibly removed to reservations in Western Oregon. Today, living descendants of these people are a part of the Confederated Tribes of Grand Ronde Community of Oregon (grandronde.org) and the Confederated Tribes of the Siletz Indians (ctsi.nsn.us).

Cataloging-in-publication data is available from the Library of Congress.

ISBN 978-1-962645-05-8 paperback; ISBN 978-1-962645-06-5 ebook

♾ This paper meets the requirements of ANSI/NISO Z39.48-1992 (Permanence of Paper).

Oregon State University
OSU Press

Oregon State University Press
121 The Valley Library
Corvallis OR 97331-4501
541-737-3166 • fax 541-737-3170
www.osupress.oregonstate.edu

For my parents, Sagoro and Matsu Ito Asai, who lived extraordinary lives and lived them well, and whose influence on our lives continues long after their deaths more than fifty years ago. Through nonverbal interest in our activities, encouragement in our efforts, and instruction through the model of their day-to-day lives, they continue to enrich our lives today. It is likely their unspoken hopes were that we would have a positive effect on our fellow human beings.

As the eighth and last of their children, I further dedicate this book to the third, fourth, and fifth generations of this family, in the hope that they will understand and appreciate the rich legacy left to them by my parents.

Contents

Preface

This book is the personal story of an American child of Japanese immigrants, an effort to further record a family history introduced previously with my 1990 book, *Made in Japan and Settled in Oregon*. It is a story told and retold more than fifty times in as many years, to students from fourth grade through university as well as to adults and seniors.

Considerable time and effort were expended by my sons to edit, revise, and enrich the story, and I much appreciate that commitment. They too have heard this story many times over the decades, reliving and resharing our family reminiscences. Their monumental tasks of questioning me, clearing up details of incidents mentioned in my previous book, adding facts and stories to answer readers' questions, and sharing the story with their many cousins as well as with the general public are not left unnoticed. Thank you.

Mitzi Asai Loftus

I was less than half my current age in the early or mid-1980s when my mother showed me the handwritten draft of an account she was writing for her children and our cousins. She said she wanted members of the third generation of our family to know their grandparents better, and to take pride in our heritage. As she spoke to high school and university students over the years, however, she became aware that people outside the family were also interested in the story and desired to know more. A budding copy editor and proofreader at the time, I helped her clean up and expand the manuscript, and in due course, it was published in 1990 as *Made in Japan and Settled in Oregon.*

Over the ensuing quarter century, we heard more stories from Mom that had not been included in her book. Rereading it, I also realized that someone who knows nothing about the Japanese American incarceration might not grasp the distinctions between the various camps to which the Asai family was sent. Mom's account meandered back and forth between experiences in three separate camps—Fresno, Tule Lake, and Heart Mountain—each with a different purpose, detainee population, and "camp culture."

I proposed to revise the book and, with my brother Toby gathering and scanning archival family photographs, to get it republished. Though the story is not substantially different, it is more detailed and supported by additional content from secondary sources. The greatest differences and additions to the story appear in chapters 7–12, which discuss World War II, the camps, and how her hometown treated Mom after she returned to Hood River.

Toby and I agreed this account deserved a new title and cover art to distinguish it from the 1990 version. *From Thorns to Blossoms* is the result. We are pleased that Oregon State University Press elected to publish it.

David Loftus

CHAPTER I

What Are You?

"What are you, Mitzi?"

I cannot count the number of times I have been asked that question, especially in my adult life. Children do not ask. They may wonder silently or simply assume. When this question is asked of me in the United States, I answer "Japanese," because I know the questioner wants to know what my racial or national origin is. My parents both had round eyes and high cheekbones, more like Native Americans than the stereotypical Japanese with almond-shaped eyes and a small, flat nose.

Although by American standards I have a small, flat nose, my nose is large enough that elder Japanese peers of my parents used to remark about me as a child, "My, she has a 'high' nose! Just like the *hakujins* [Caucasian Americans]!"

When the question was asked of me in Europe, I always answered, "American," an unsatisfactory response to the questioners. "No, no, not American," they would say. Then I would add, "My father and my mother are Japanese who came to America, but I was born in the United States. Therefore I am Japanese American." That was the explanation they wanted. "OK, American," they would concede.

In Japan, people are taught that it is not polite to ask such questions until one has known someone for a long time. In my yearlong stay in Japan as a Fulbright teacher in 1957-58, I was sure that various glances betrayed a desire to ask. As soon as I stepped onto a train or bus, eyes turned curiously upon me. Although I seemed to be Japanese and could understand and speak the language, people were confused by my rural speech, my mien, and carriage. The body language and "cultural personality" were not Japanese. If I had told them I was Japanese, they would demand the same explanation I gave the Europeans.

Among the Warm Springs Indians in Oregon, I was a guest every April for several years in the 1980s along with all the American Field Service high school exchange students in the state. Since 1947, AFS has sponsored the travel of hundreds of thousands of US and foreign high school students around the world.[1] In the 1970s, '80s, and '90s, my husband and I hosted students from France, Israel, New Zealand, Spain, and Vietnam. My Warm Springs hosts never asked, "What are you?" Instead, it was, "What tribe are you from, Mitzi?" Despite painstakingly explaining my Japanese heritage, two days later, as I prepared to leave the reservation, various elders of the tribe asked, "Now, what tribe did you say you are from, Mitzi?"

One year at the reservation, I was seated on the bus with an exchange student from Japan after tribal members had told us about their religion. This boy was a convert to the Latter-Day Saints church. He asked me many questions about Indian religion. Finally, I told him that I could not answer his questions because I did not know any more about their religion than he did.

"Well, what tribe do you belong to? Do you have a different religion?" he asked.

"What tribe?" I replied with surprise. "I'm not Indian. I'm Japanese."

"Japanese?" he responded skeptically.

"Yes, Japanese. One hundred percent," I stated proudly.

"One hundred percent?!" he said even more incredulously.

"My father was born in Aichi Prefecture, and my mother was born in Mie Prefecture. They came to America at the turn of the century and lived here the rest of their lives," I explained. I even spoke some Japanese and recounted my experiences as an English teacher in Japan, and still he looked dubious about my heritage.

Other AFS exchange students also assumed that I was one of the Warm Springs Native Americans, instead of just an adult AFS volunteer. After the Powwow, lectures, and demonstrations by the Native Americans, many of them came up to thank me. I merely replied, "You're welcome!" I went to the reservation for several years and gave up trying to convince the Native Americans that I am Japanese American, and the Japanese that I am not Native American.

The first time my husband's parents met my parents, they remarked on how much my parents looked like the Eskimos (now properly identified as Athabascans) in Alaska. Since most of my friends and acquaintances knew that my husband Don was born in Fairbanks and had lived there until graduating from high school, Don often teasingly introduced me as his "Eskimo wife"—and they believed him.

I have been thought to be Chinese, Hawaiian, and East Indian, but most often American Indian. Japanese was at best only the third or fourth guess.

Our eldest son has perhaps the most Asian characteristics of our three sons. When David was 10 years old, our family traveled to Morocco. The Moroccans looked first at Don (Norwegian-German-English), then at me (Japanese), and finally at David. They put an arm around his shoulders, nodded approvingly, and pointed at him, saying, "*Maroc* [He's Moroccan]!"

Our second son, Kenneth, has seldom been identified as half-Asian. He was startled when, in his senior year in college, he was

The Don Loftus family in Coos Bay, 1972: from left, Don, David, Ken, Mitzi, and Toby (Loftus family collection)

approached by a Japanese boy and asked, "Pardon me, but are you by chance part Japanese?" He traveled in Europe at age 18 and again when he was 20. In Spain, he was often taken to be Spanish. When Ken and his AFS exchange student "brother," Davíd Rodriguez Peralto, were together, strangers would ask Ken for directions or information. When the two boys traveled together across Europe, Ken was taken for the Spaniard, and Davíd of Spain was thought to be the American, especially in Finland. Ken was assumed to be Finnish!

In the summer of 1982, I was visiting Linares, Spain, during the town festival. Davíd's father arranged for Ken to be awarded a trophy for dancing the Sevillana (Andalucian regional dance done during the festival especially) after several days of dancing with various Spanish girls as partners. During all these dances, Ken had never spoken. When the trophy was presented to him, and the last word on the inscription was read—*norteamericano*—there were many astonished Spanish girls, as evidenced by the number of hands that rose to cover mouths and the look of surprise in their eyes.

As far as I know, our third son, Toby, has never been thought to be anything but "American."

After asking "What are you?" questioners want to know, "Where did you come from?" This book tells the story in the best way that I am able, drawing from childhood memories, family conversations, and help from my late brothers and sister. The answer must begin with my parents, to whom all of us children referred as Pa and Ma.

These were endearing terms, but they were never used in direct address to them, only as names we used to refer to them when talking about them. When we spoke directly to them, we usually called them Papa and Mama.

CHAPTER 2

Pa and Ma in the New World

Pa was born Sagoro Asai on January 25, 1880, in Inamoto Village, Aichi Prefecture, Japan. Today, Inamoto is an urban neighborhood of Yatomi, a suburb about 23 miles west of Nagoya, Japan's fourth-largest city. It is near the Pacific Coast (east side) and roughly in the center of Japan, about 265 kilometers or 164 miles west of Tokyo; and northeast of Kyoto (91 miles) and Osaka (110 miles).

Pa was born at a time of great change. Thomas Edison had invented the incandescent lamp in 1879, and Alexander Graham Bell invented the telephone in 1880. It would be many years before the house Pa built in America would have either, though.

A phone was not installed in our home until after World War II, when I was in junior high school. What an exciting event that was, although I was not allowed to use the telephone for social calls until later.

Not long after Pa's arrival in the United States in 1904, radio was invented. The Kodak camera, automobile, and airplane were all introduced within the first thirty years of Pa's life. A time of great change indeed, but these impressive inventions were not universally adopted or accepted. Pa was wary of airplanes and would not travel on one until the 1960s. After his first plane ride (to Japan) he remarked, "It's smoother than a car ride, and my coffee didn't even spill!" He made at least two other plane trips to Japan after that.

I remember when I was a little girl in the 1930s, my older brothers would lie in bed listening to Jack Benny, Fred Allen, *The Great Gildersleeve*, *Suspense*, *Gang Busters*, Charlie McCarthy and Edgar Bergen, *Your Hit Parade*, *The Shadow*, *The Green Hornet*, and other weekly radio programs.

We owned a Kodak camera with a leather accordion pull-out lens, an item that was confiscated from us during the World War II years. We also had a Model T Ford, which barely ran and was parked in the barnyard. Once in a while, we children would push this car downhill from our house and coast a mile down the road, hoping that it would start or that we could get it crank-started to drive back home up the hill.

Later, Pa bought a new 1937 Chrysler, for cash. We chose this model after the whole family, all nine of us, went to town to get "fitted" for a car. The Chrysler had the most room, so a Chrysler it was.

Pa was the second son in his family, which meant that he had no hope of inheriting the family farm. In such cases, men married into a family of all girls. By marrying the eldest daughter of such a family, a man would take on the wife's family name and thereby become the "adopted" eldest son and property owner. My father did not choose this route.

Neither did he take the option of apprenticeship in some trade or business, for this would necessitate living in town or in a city, which he did not desire. Instead, he volunteered for the army, but was rejected for being too short. My father never weighed more than 130 pounds in his lifetime, measuring slightly over five feet. He was strong and wiry, and robust in health all his life. He could outdo almost any man around for good, hard physical labor. Most of the years we children were growing up, he started work a couple hours before breakfast, before the rest of us got out of bed.

Once when he was in his seventies, he cut down a tree with the help of Bob Moller, a neighbor on whose border the tree stood. Bob was in his thirties or forties at the time. They used a two-man saw, and Bob had to stop and puff several times before the job was finished, at Bob's request and with much ribbing on Pa's part.

My father said that his mother was the head of the household. His father was one of those "adopted" eldest sons who had married into her family—a family of all girls. My father loved and respected his mother, perhaps also feared her at times. His father died a drunkard. My father attributed this to the fact that his father had to live with a woman who bossed him, in a society where the man was usually the undisputed authority in most households.

Pa said his father was a kind-hearted man, a gentle soul overcome by a strong though intelligent wife. Pa loved and respected his father, too, but he believed his father had been driven to drink. Many times as a youngster, Pa had to go to the village tavern to lead, coax, or carry his father home. After one such occasion, his father, upon returning home, asked Pa to hold him in his lap. My father did so. His father asked him to shift him around several times, to try to get him into a more comfortable position. No matter how hard he tried, his father was not satisfied. His father died in his arms that night. Pa was 18 and his father around 40. Pa recounted this experience time and again. How deep an impression this must have made on him.

All his life, Pa was much opposed to drinking, although he always kept a bottle of Four Roses bourbon on hand, which he used as a remedy when he felt a cold coming on. He served alcohol to his alcohol-loving friends, for in Japanese culture, one seldom imposes his own beliefs, values, or prejudices on guests. An effort is made to give pleasure, comfort, and hospitality to visitors.

As for his own tolerance for alcohol, one drink would make him red-faced and send him to bed or down for a nap. He smoked cigarettes for many years as a young man, but he gave up smoking in the 1930s, after he suffered an unusually bad cold during a flu epidemic. In my lifetime, therefore, I remember him as a nonsmoker.

Having been refused by the military, Pa decided there would be little to lose and a great possible adventure to be gained by going to America, so he "sought his fortune in the golden land of opportunity." In 1904, he asked his mother for his share of the family funds, an amount I cannot accurately recall today. It was something less than a hundred dollars; enough for boat passage to America and not much else.

A "Manifest of Alien Passengers for the U.S. Immigration Officer at Port of Arrival" states that Sagoro Asai, age 24, departed Yokohama aboard the steamship *Coptic* on May 23, 1904.[1] It notes that he could read and write, and was carrying three dollars on him. Among checklist items on the printed manifest was whether each alien passenger was "Deformed or crippled," had ever been "in prison or almshouse," or was "a Polygamist" or "an Anarchist." As for every other passenger, the columns for my father all have "no" written in them. The ship arrived at the port of Honolulu sometime in June before sailing on to San Francisco, where Pa disembarked.

In 1897, Thomas Edison filmed several thirty-second shorts of the *Coptic* in one of his early movies in 1897, now stored in the Library of Congress.[2] It's unlikely Pa knew about the ship's history, but that first trip from Japan to the United States in 1904 was the most memorable of all the voyages Pa was to make across the Pacific Ocean in his sixty-odd years of life in America. The people were crowded into the bottom of the ship with no compartments, no beds, no circulation, and no privacy. Like animals in the hold, they were crowded, sleeping on the floor and sharing everything—especially sickness and lice. Pa fortunately remained healthy throughout the trip and spent most of his time helping others who were ill, homesick, seasick, and depressed. In his own words, "It was just like a cattle ship."

Pa was one of many millions who came to the United States during this period. From 1836 to 1914, more than 30 million Europeans—mostly Germans, Italians, Spanish, Swedish, and Russians—immigrated to the United States.[3] In the 1880s, almost 1.5 million came from Germany alone.[4] They were for the most part welcomed, accepted, and eventually granted citizenship.

But their Asian counterparts remained social and legal aliens for decades. The first Japanese to immigrate to the United States settled east of Sacramento, California, in 1869.[5] A year later, Congress granted naturalization rights to "free whites and peoples of African descent." Asians were conspicuously absent.[6]

In 1913, California passed the Alien Land Law, which barred foreigners from owning land in that state.[7] Pa bought his first piece of land in 1911, but by the time he sought to make a second purchase, Oregon had passed its own version, which prohibited Japanese and Chinese nationals from buying and leasing land, and even operating farm machinery.[8] Pa registered the property in the name of "Asai Brothers," my two eldest brothers, who were about 5 and 3 years old at the time. Pa was legal guardian of the property, and when my brothers were in their twenties, the full ownership papers were drawn up in their names.

Pa started farming at a time when the slant-eyed, buck-toothed, bespectacled stereotype of the Japanese was popularized. Japanese were depicted as sly, deceitful villains with intentions of taking over California. Many political cartoons featured these caricatures in the 1930s and '40s. The Hearst newspapers published articles and cartoons expressing fear and dislike of the new Asian residents in California. V. S. McClatchy, co-owner and publisher of the *Sacramento Bee*, withdrew from the newspaper business to form the California Joint Immigration Committee, a small group intended to defend California against the "yellow peril."[9] He appeared before a US Senate committee to warn of the economic threat the Japanese posed for the United States. Other groups, such as the

Japanese Exclusion League of California, organized to protest the immigration of Japanese to the United States. Similar groups had worked to exclude Chinese immigrants forty years earlier.

Their efforts were successful, as the Immigration Act of 1924 ended all immigration from Japan.[10] This would be the law of the land for decades. The Immigration Act of 1952 finally ended Asian exclusion (although, in practice, extremely limited quotas still effectively prevented Japanese immigration) and granted citizenship eligibility to nonwhite immigrants.[11] By then, Pa had lived in the United States for forty-eight years and was 72 years old. More than another decade passed before the Immigration and Nationality Act officially did away with the racist and discriminatory quota system, in 1965,[12] which opened the way for significantly larger numbers of immigrants from Asia.

After Pa arrived in San Francisco, he went to work building railroads. A middleman hired immigrants, gave them a place to sleep and food to eat, and like indentured servants, they had to work off those costs before they could keep what money they earned. Some of the stories Pa told of his struggles with the English language during his early days as a bachelor in a strange country were filled with humor. He was bewildered by the many chiding remarks made to the men on the railroad section gang to "get the ants out of your pants," to "step on it," to "get the lead out," and other such slang and idiomatic expressions.

My father was tabbed immediately as having a sense of humor and thus became the butt of many a practical joke. Once he returned from the store and inquired what "two betch" was worth; the store clerk had quoted that amount, and he did not know what it meant. The fellows winked at each other over this great opportunity to play another joke on "Sam," as they came to call him. One man answered, "Oh, two betch is twenty-five cents; four betch is fifty cents; six betch is seventy-five cents; and a son-of-a-betch is a dollar." Pa went out to use his newly acquired English and soon learned that they had "pulled his leg," to use another expression he had to master. Since he could not pronounce "son-of-a," it came out "son-a-ka"—so perhaps the storekeeper did not understand him in more ways than one.

Back then, a person could not usually go into a store and pick out the items he wanted by hand. More often, he had to tell the storekeeper just what he wanted, and the storekeeper would gather the goods together behind the counter or in a back room. Americans expected good use of language and did not make things easier for a foreigner, the way they tend to do more nowadays. Many times Pa went to the store armed with stones so that he could cackle like a hen, drop the stones, and put up his fingers to indicate how many eggs he wanted to buy.

After working on the railroad in California and Oregon, Pa saved enough money to buy some land. In his travels with the railroad, he had kept a keen eye out for land that looked good for farming. In Hood River, Oregon, he found what suited both him and his pocketbook. He quit the railroad and purchased twenty acres of cheap, marginal land in 1911. That original homestead is about five miles southwest from the farm where I would be born two decades later. It was up the Hood River Valley near Ditch Creek between the town and Mount Hood.

Using a horse, dynamite, and hand tools, Pa built a road a quarter mile up a slope and cleared the property. He cut down the timber and sold it off, dynamited the stumps, and planted fruit trees. The house he built was rough, uninsulated, cold, and uncomfortable. It was made of crudely fitted boards, with cracks in the walls that let in cold air, daylight, moisture, and bugs. A wood-fueled kitchen stove provided what heat it could. Six of my seven older brothers and sisters would be born there. (I believe Dick, the next oldest child to me, was born at an intermediate home closer to town, and I was born in the house in the valley that remains with the family today.)

Pa was 31. I believe he was among the first ten Japanese immigrants to settle in Hood River. Most of them were single men who in the next few years were to bring Japanese wives to the valley. The 1910 US Census identifies S. Asai, age 31, as "Hired Man" and "Farm Hand," and erroneously lists his year of immigration as 1902.[13] Of the forty-nine other individuals listed on the same page of the census (and presumably living nearby), twelve are listed as native Japanese, three from Germany, one from Canada, and one from England. No other foreigners are noted. Ten years later, the 1920 Census would list seven native Finns in the Oak Grove Precinct near the Asai farm.[14]

Since he had grown only rice in Japan, Pa knew nothing about fruit orchards. He worked for other ranchers to gain experience in fruit farming and earn enough money to prepare his acreage for the bearing stage. This took seven years, since faster-bearing dwarf and semidwarf fruit trees had not yet been developed. One farm for which Pa worked in Hood River was owned by a man named Horace Manuel. Native Japanese speakers' difficulty separating the English "L" from the "R"—because the most equivalent consonant sound in Japanese is somewhere between the two—has long been a source of humor for British and American comics. The name of Pa's employer on this farm posed a special challenge; from my father's mouth, it came out something like "Ho-wuss Mahnua"—almost like he was saying "horse manure"!

When Pa worked for the Manuels, he lived in an upstairs room of their home. They fed him meals and otherwise treated him as a member of the household. Each morning, Pa would eat a large number of pancakes.

Unlike the railroad section gang where he worked before this time, Sundays were not workdays. In those early days, Pa was not familiar with the American custom of eating only two meals on Sundays (late breakfast or brunch and Sunday dinner in middle or late afternoon). He was a heavy eater and worked very hard (the best worker they had ever had), so Mr. Manuel had encouraged Pa to eat all he wanted the rest of the week. The first Sunday he lived at the Manuels', he rose early as usual and waited in his room to be called for breakfast. He got hungrier and hungrier, and when they had not called him yet at nine o'clock, he began to worry.

Was his work not satisfactory? Were the Manuels sick? He finally went downstairs to ask when breakfast would be, and the farmer said, "Oh, did you want to eat breakfast as usual today, too?" The cultural misunderstanding was cleared up, they cooked a big batch of pancakes, and Pa ate twenty-three of them, stocking up in anticipation of having only one more meal that day.

He then wrote to his mother and eldest brother in Japan and declared that he was ready for them to pick out a wife for him. In Japan, it was common for marriages to be arranged between the parents of the parties involved. It still happens today: an American Field Service classmate of my youngest son Toby, Mikio, had one in the late 1990s because he seldom dated and was still unmarried in his late twenties. His parents made the arrangements. A century ago, the men were often in their thirties and their wives 18 to 20 years old. In the case of immigrants, there was no other option if one desired a wife from the "old country." The expanse of the Pacific Ocean and the enormous cost of returning to Japan compelled young men to depend on their parents' good judgment.

Mr. Manuel asked Pa why he would choose a Japanese wife over an American woman. His reply was, "Well, I notice that you get up first in the morning, start the fire, put on the coffee, and when your wife gets up, you have to help her with her corset strings. None of that for me!" His employer laughed and had to admit that my father had a point. Many of us have speculated as to how my father happened to know that Mr. Manuel had to help his wife with her corset strings, but it makes a good story in any case. It never occurred to me to ask him for an explanation.

My grandmother in Japan sent him the pictures of several girls, carefully screened by her, any one of whom would make a good wife for Pa. From these pictures, he chose my mother, Matsu Ito, to be his bride. Born on October 17, 1892, she had grown up in Kisosaki, a village on the Kiso River, barely a mile west of Pa's village of Inamoto. They had seen each other once or twice as children, but that was the extent of their acquaintance. Since my mother was twelve years younger than Pa, she could not have been more than 12 years of age when he left Japan.

My mother sailed aboard the *Kamakura Maru* on July 19, 1911, according to the ship's manifest, and arrived in Seattle on either August 3 or 4, 1911.[15] An immigration card shows both dates. The card also lists a distinguishing mark of "A mole on the neck," "85" in money shown, and identifies her occupation as "Housewife." She is also identified on both the ship manifest and immigration card as Matsu Asai, even though she was not yet married to my father.[16]

Ma was not quite 19 years old. My parents told me there were thirty-nine other women bound for the United States to become picture brides aboard the ship. This was but one of several such loads of precious cargo to Japanese bachelors on the US mainland. What was in the minds and hearts of forty men and forty women as that boat sailed across the Pacific?

It was not until years later, when my mother was in her sixties or seventies, that we learned how she had felt about coming to a strange country to marry a man she did not know. My mother-in-law, Dorothy Loftus—who my husband Don said was like a lawyer, inquiring about your whole history in the first thirty minutes after meeting you—asked my mother, "How did you feel about coming to a strange country where you couldn't speak the language, and you didn't know the man you were going to marry?"

She answered, "I didn't want to." Pa's mother had paid her parents a visit and made the proposal. My mother refused. In traditional Japanese culture, a girl did not have a right to express her

Grandmother Asai, Pa's mother (Asai family collection)

own feelings in such matters. She could have been labeled a libertine, but somehow this does not accurately describe the mother I knew. I realized how liberal her family must have been back in 1911, since they asked her if she would like to marry this man in America.

Her future mother-in-law (a domineering woman) came three times to Ma's house to appeal to her. On the final visit, she got down on her hands and knees, shed tears, and begged my mother to go to America to be her son's wife. Her persistence paid off; my mother relented and said, "Oh well, all right, then."

Pa had written his bride-to-be and instructed her not to bring any clothes—work or dress—except what was on her back and whatever else she needed to make the trip. More important, she was to bring two futon, the heavy, thick bed quilt commonly used in Japan. My mother followed his instructions to the letter, which says something about her personality.

Without bringing any clothes with her, what did she wear in America? Perhaps like the thirty-nine other bachelors, Pa had paid an entrepreneur a flat fee of fifty dollars for a trousseau, which consisted of a long white linen dress, long white gloves, a parasol, high-buttoned shoes, a wide-brimmed hat, and a corset—just what a farmer's wife needed.

Pa waved a green flag on the shore so Matsu could pick him out from the other expectant grooms. My parents were married less than twenty-four hours after Ma got off the boat, at the Buddhist Church in Seattle by Hoshin Fujii, on August 4, 1911.[17] When my parents went to be married, they were asked to present a ring, so Pa trotted over to the nearest dime store for a token ring to use for the ceremony. The ring turned Ma's finger green in a few days, so she threw it away. She wore her corset a couple of times, but it was too tight and confining, so she threw it in the trunk and forgot all about it. How I wish I had possession of it now!

Ma's name, Matsu, is a traditionally masculine name that means "pine tree." It was common in those years for parents to give both boys and girls masculine names. Infant mortality was high, and people thought that by giving a baby a boy's name, it might be stronger and have a greater chance of survival. My father's older brother by six years, Rikimatsu, and his wife had eleven children, but six of them died before the age of 3. At any rate, Matsu enjoyed unusually good health and strength most of her life.

Before Ma and Pa were united in marriage, a slight error had to be corrected. (Thank heavens Pa was as persistent a man as his mother before him.) Another bachelor named Mr. Arai was also waiting for his bride to disembark from the ship. Because of the similarity of the names Asai and Arai, Mr. Arai's bride was presented to my father. Pa looked at the woman and refused to accept her, for he was sure she was not the bride he had chosen from the selection of photos his mother had sent him.

Pa took his new bride to Hood River, where they lived for fifty-five years—less three years during the war, when our family was placed in prison camps along with 120,000 other Japanese and Japanese Americans, including the Arais, who resided in the same block of the camp. The two families got together and laughed about the name confusion in Seattle back in 1911, and speculated what might have happened if Pa had not been adamant. The children would all certainly have had different faces from those we knew in the 1940s.

When my mother left Japan to be a picture bride in the United States, her youngest brother Shōemon was around 13 years old. Just before she left, he ran to the rice paddies and gathered up worms or bugs, which were boiled into a broth for my mother to drink. It was thought that this concoction would ensure a life of good health. For this favor, her brother asked her to send him a gift from America. Not many years after she had settled in Oregon, she sent him a silver pocket watch with a cover that snapped shut over its face.

When I visited Japan in 1957, I saw this pocket watch at my uncle's house. At the time he had received it, forty-six years before, few people in his village owned a timepiece of any kind, and it became a source of pride and prestige to him that villagers would ask him, a young man of 18 or so, for the time of day. He told me that the watch had run for thirteen years, after which he tried in vain to have it repaired. Since it was an American watch, the parts needed to repair it were not available. For many years afterward, my uncle kept the precious gift in the bottom drawer of the Buddhist altar of worship, a sort of wardrobe closet affair with doors that shut, often the only piece of furniture visible in a typical Japanese farmer's combination living-dining-bedroom. I have kicked myself several times for lacking the presence of mind to take the watch and have it repaired for my uncle.

CHAPTER 3

Return Visit to Japan

By an interesting coincidence, my parents' first child, a girl named Masako, was born on Pa's 32nd birthday in 1913. Masako would reside in the United States only three years. Two and a half years after Masako, a son, Taro, was born. I knew him as "Tot" all my life. A second coincidence is that Ma and Pa's third child, Masami, always known to us as "Min," was born on Ma's birthday in 1917, although his birth was preceded by my parents' first trip back to Japan.

My parents described that return visit to Japan together in early 1916 with their two eldest children as being more pleasant than Pa's first trip to America. They were crowded together in communal fashion as before, however. Ma told me that she took a trunk full of rags on that trip. It took two weeks to reach Japan, and she used the rags as diapers, which Pa would heave overboard each day to save washing them. I suspect there were probably no facilities aboard for washing them anyway. The empty diaper trunk was filled with souvenirs and purchases in Japan for the return trip.

My uncles and aunts in Japan were fascinated by my parents' visit. I heard them tell these stories when I went to Japan to teach English more than forty years later in 1957-58. It was a romantic description of a woman I did not recognize as the mother I knew.

Ma, Pa, baby Taro, and Masako about 1915 (Asai family collection)

Ma's youngest sister said, "Oh, but she was elegant! She had rings on her fingers, high-buttoned shoes, long white gloves, a large-brimmed hat, a linen dress that went down to her ankles, parasol," and perhaps unbeknownst to my aunt, a corset. Yes, Ma was wearing the outfit purchased in Seattle by Pa as a trousseau from the picture-bride entrepreneur.

At that point, Ma's second child was a nursing baby. She told me years later that like most women at the time, she nursed all of her babies until they were two years old. During the trip to her home village in Japan, Ma learned of a starving infant whose mother was not able to produce enough milk. Ma offered herself as a wet nurse and breast-fed the emaciated child along with her own baby. Unfortunately, the starving baby was too far gone and died anyway. Ma felt very bad about this.

My paternal grandmother, the one who had begged Ma to marry Pa five years before, was in poor health at this time and well along in years. This was the main reason for my parents' trip back to Japan. My grandmother argued that since 3-year-old Masako was a girl, she would only be a burden on the farm in the United States and not much help as a farm worker, the way a boy might be. Leaving her in Japan would free Ma to work harder, unencumbered by a "useless baby daughter."

In Ma's mind, a dying grandmother's suggestion was practically a command, so my parents left Masako with her grandmother, but not without grief on Ma's part, as I was to learn many years later. Asked much later how she felt about leaving her firstborn child in Japan, Ma indicated it had been a difficult and heartbreaking thing to do. She did not want to do it, but she felt her desires must be subordinated to those of her mother-in-law, and she resigned herself to it. This is a natural Japanese adjustment pattern. Resignation is a fact of life in Japanese culture, expressed in the phrase *Shikataganai* ("it can't be helped"). The phrase and the philosophy it expressed would figure prominently during World War II and the mass imprisonment of Japanese immigrants and their children on the West Coast.

Masako was never to return to the United States. Since seven other children came along in the next sixteen years, Ma and Pa had little time, money, or freedom to go to Japan and fetch their oldest child home. A maiden aunt, Joko, Pa's eldest sister, treated Masako as her own child. This aunt lived on the old home farm in the village of Inamoto all her life and died there at age 70.

Never in all my childhood was I aware of Ma's deep hurt over losing Masako, because she never showed her feelings enough for a young child to notice. I do remember her crying softly a few times after she learned that Masako had died in 1945, a fact we did not learn until a year after it happened. (That story will be related in chapter 13.) To a girl of 13 or 14 years, those were simple tears shed by anyone at any person's death, for death had little meaning to me then. Three more years passed before death came close enough to touch me personally, when my brother Half died. Even then, Ma's personal sense of loss over Masako did not occur to me.

The ship's manifest for the *Mexico Maru* of the Osaka Shoshen Kaisha line, which departed Yokohama on February 13, 1916, reflects the absence of my parents' firstborn: it lists Sagoro Asai, 36 years, 1 month; Matsu Asai, 23 years, 4 months; and Taro Asai, 7 months.[1] My father and mother are each identified as a "Nonimmigrant."

Ma described the conglomeration of people who boarded the ship at various ports of call on the return trip from Japan. Many Russians were fleeing their country at this time, shortly before the Russian Revolution, and Ma recalled seeing many of them on this voyage. One in particular gave her cause to be nervous. A young Russian girl, though unable to communicate in any common language, expressed an eagerness to hold my mother's baby and to play with him during the day.

Ma dreaded the thought and did her best to avoid any contact with the girl, but at the same time she did not want to be rude. One night, when all the ship passengers were asleep, Ma was awakened by strange snapping and popping noises. The Russian girl had removed her clothes and held a small candle by her side. She was killing body lice, which were readily exposed and spotted at night. Arrival cards dated March 1, 1916, state that my father stepped off the boat at the port of Seattle accompanied by "wife & child," but the card for my mother says only "husb."[2]

I often refer to the approximate age of persons because birthdays in Japan were not celebrated according to the Gregorian calendar as they are in the United States (which is still widely the case today). When those of Pa and Ma's generation spoke about their age, they never referred to the month, day, and year but rather said, "He was born in the second year of Meiji," or "I was born in the first year of Taishō." (These refer to the reigns of the emperors of Japan through the turn of the last century: Meiji from 1867 to 1912, and Taishō from 1923 to 1926.)

All birthdays were celebrated on New Year's Day, which explains why that holiday is such an important one for Japanese people. They kept track of their ages only as a relative matter. "We are the same age because were both born in the fourth year of Meiji."

When we children tried to remember and celebrate our parents' birthdays, there was always an argument as to which birthday it was and how old Ma or Pa really were. For these reasons, Pa and Ma understandably lost track of the years of their marriage and celebrated their golden wedding anniversary six months late. They held off because they thought they had been married only forty-nine years. Every January, all resident aliens were required to report to the post office. The year of their anniversary, my parents realized from the dates on their alien registration cards that they had lost track of a year, and the golden wedding anniversary celebration was pushed up to February, when in fact they had been married fifty years the preceding August.

I believe Pa sent money to his brother Rikimatsu, in whose home Masako spent most of her growing years, to pay for her to return to Oregon. Her grandmother had long since died, not long after my parents left their daughter in Japan. Having grown up and gone to school with friends there, Masako was not eager to be sent to a "foreign" land, and her uncle did not push her. For this Pa was critical of his brother. "He does not possess the necessary 'starch' to handle such matters," he said of the matter.

In 1934-35, Ma paid another visit to Japan, this time accompanied by my eldest brother Taro ("Tot"), the baby of the first trip who was now in school; 5-year-old Itsu, my brother just three years older than I and who we called "Dick"; and me. I have pictures of us standing on the deck of the ship with Masako, but I was too

On ship during 1935 visit to Japan: (rear row) Tot, Ma, Masako, and Aunt O-no; (front row) Mitsuko (me) and Itsuo ("Dick") (Asai family collection)

young to have any memory of her. She was about 22 at that point and a stranger to me.

Masako did not return to the United States with us that time, either. Although my parents had hoped that she would return to America, Masako successfully resisted their efforts to bring her back. In that sense Ma and Pa were already Americanized, because the Japanese way would have been to enforce the decision without Masako's input and compel her to live with them in the United States. Instead, they respected her wishes and left her in Japan.

If Pa had been along on the trip, it is possible that he might have insisted on her return. Ma was a timid, gentle lady. If her husband's family said no to the plan, she probably did not resist. The only answer I ever got from Pa and Ma as to why Masako never returned was that she did not want to come.

Timepieces seem to crop up in this family saga. Ma told a story about Dick on that trip. As a 5-year-old, he could tell time, and other passengers on the boat delighted in sending him to look at the ship's clock over and over again.

Another story from this voyage (one Tot quickly grew tired of) was about his walking on the tatami mats in a Buddhist temple in his street shoes. The Japanese remove their footwear at the entry of any building or home, but when Tot went to his cousin's house in Fukude-machi, Shizuoka Prefecture, he walked right into the house and the temple without removing his shoes.

His cousin Yaeko married the priest of this temple, Ryoken, and their house is attached to the temple. The story about Tot and the tatami was told to me again in 1957 by my Buddhist priest cousin, twenty years after it happened. Little did he know how many times I had already heard that story back in Oregon. The American relatives seemed like foreigners to my Japanese relatives. I probably seemed foreign to them when I first met them in 1957-58, but we were kindred spirits nonetheless.

The priest Ryoken died in the 1960s, succeeded by his son-in-law, Genpō, who was succeeded by grandson Genshō.

CHAPTER 4

"Midhusband" and Parenting Eight Children

Those early days of struggling to eke out a living from the land, and of rearing a family of eight children, produced many great family anecdotes.

On the hillside farm, my parents grew asparagus on a steep slope. At the top of the slope was a flat area where fruit trees grew. One cold and icy winter, Pa was walking at the top of this hill, surveying his apple trees. He slipped on an icy spot and slid down the hill, gaining momentum as he went. The road he had built up to his ranch bordered it at the lower end of the asparagus patch, and he was sliding so fast that he flew right across the road and farther down toward the Hood River, which flowed several hundred yards below the ranch.

Fortunately, he slowed to a stop at a large level area before he reached the water. He remembered the neighbors making a stretcher out of a board and blanket to carry him back up the steep and slippery climb to his home. In the accident he injured his face, resulting in a permanent scar. On another occasion, he had a close call with dynamite as he was removing stumps of old trees. This left him with a facial scar, too. In the local newspaper, the *Hood River News*, the story of Pa's fall down the icy slope was reprinted from time to time in columns that listed incidents from the past.

Ma and Pa in hillside orchard with Masaaki ("Half"), Mika in arms, Min, and Tot, about 1923 (Asai family collection)

Pa delivered all but one of his eight children himself, and we always used to say, "How did Pa do that? He can't even find a can opener in the kitchen!" Ma would work side by side with Pa in the orchard during pregnancy and then give birth to a child, put it on her back the next day, and continue working beside Pa. She said with a laugh, "After a few babies, he got soft-hearted, however, and let me stay home a couple of days!"

I don't believe Pa required Ma to work so soon. Ma did this voluntarily as her own idea of what was expected of her. After he had delivered one or two babies, he could accurately predict when childbirth was imminent. Ma would be working near him, and as her time drew near, he would keep a close watch on Ma's face. He could tell when the time had come, and he would send her home to lie down. Then he would go home himself after working a couple more hours and deliver the child, who usually appeared according to Pa's confident timetable.

Pa said Ma had a great craving for oranges during one of her pregnancies. He made a special trip to town (more than ten miles by horse and wagon) to buy a sack of oranges for her. When he brought them home, she ate every one of the oranges in one sitting, which made him feel sorry he had not gotten them sooner. Ma would sit and laugh softly with embarrassment whenever Pa told this story about her.

Those early winters in Hood River were more severe than most people have known in the century since. Snow fell every year and stayed. The rural-route mailbox was a good four miles from our house. The mail was not often picked up for days at a time, but on the day that a new baby arrived, you can be sure that the mailbox was checked. Pa would bundle up and send all the children off to the mailbox while he and Ma got ready for another childbirth session. It was Pa's belief that his old maid sister in Japan had been frightened for life after viewing childbirth as a girl. He felt sure that a young woman especially should never witness a baby's birth until after giving birth to a child herself.

In spite of Pa's precautions to keep childbirth from view of his children, his fears that irreparable psychological harm would come from it may have been unfounded. Ma told of having observed a woman undergo childbirth in Japan before Ma came to the United States to be married. Most Japanese farmhouses had a room designated for childbirth, she said. In that room would be a hook or some device on the ceiling to which a rope could be attached. The rope hung down within reach of the woman, who was half-standing, half-crouching. Knots tied in the rope allowed her to get a good hold. Two other women would support her in the delivery.

In vertical fashion, the lady was delivered of her baby, with the help of a midwife and an assistant. Ma served as errand girl to fetch hot water, rags, and any other things called for. Having experienced this, she was to give birth to eight babies herself. Those births in Japan, as well as all of Ma's deliveries, were done without the benefit of anesthetics. Natural childbirth was all they knew.

My brother Masaaki ("Half") was Ma's fourth child, born in 1920. He gave Pa considerable anxiety because he was a breech baby. When Pa first realized this, he said it made him break out in a cold sweat. Ma sensed that something was out of the ordinary and asked him what was the matter. Pa did not tell her for fear it would put her in a panic. Everything came out all right in the end, including my brother, who turned out to be perhaps the most acute-minded and certainly the most independent member of the family.

For stubbornness, Half was a match for Pa. He was the only one of us who stood firm against Pa's orders and demands, and occasionally did just the opposite of what our father told him to. He engaged in verbal arguments with Pa, and I recall his walking out in the middle of a conversation with my father—a definite no-no in our family.

Half skipped two grades in elementary school and graduated from high school when he was 15. He was short for his age anyway, so it was no wonder that he was nicknamed "Half Pint," a name that was later shortened to Half. That name stuck until his life ended at age 29. Some knew him as "Ace" in the US Army and later at Oregon State College (now Oregon State University), perhaps as a diminished version of our family name (pronounced "AE-sigh" or "Ace-eye" by everyone in those days), but no one in our family called him that.

The fifth and last son, Itsuo or Dick, also skipped a grade and was dubbed "Quarter Pint." (He was born after my sister who didn't get left in Japan, Mika, and the fourth boy, Gene.) Both Half and Dick were adamant that I not be allowed to skip the first grade when it was suggested. My parents would normally accede to teacher recommendations, for in their book, "The teacher is always right." As a teacher myself from the 1950s on, I have often wished that other parents had the same attitude toward teachers that my parents had. I can especially remember Half talking to Pa and Ma, urging them not to agree to advance me a grade, and his urging had its effect. I was able to remain with my peers.

Having had so much experience as a midwife (or "midhusband"), Pa got called upon by neighbors to deliver babies when they had neither the will nor the courage to do it themselves. Years later, he admitted that delivering someone else's child was a more tense, anxious event because of the awesome responsibility and the lesser confidence he had in the general health of women other than his own wife, whom he knew to be sturdy and strong. He admitted to stage fright during every delivery he performed but thought he was successful in hiding these fears from those around him.

Once Pa delivered a stillborn child, and another time an infant covered with a cottage-cheese-like substance. After these births, he had no further stomach for delivering babies for other families, and thenceforth firmly refused to oversee any but his own. He remarked late in life that he did not fully realize or appreciate the good fortune of having a wife who was healthy, dependable, and regular in all her bodily functions. In Ma's case, everything went as the books and the "experts" said they should. Pa was not prepared for any variations and luckily did not encounter any.

The winter that Dick was born, in 1929, was an especially hard one. On January 29, the anniversary of President McKinley's assassination (a date that helped my parents remember Dick's birthday), my brother was born in subzero weather. Pa said that he had to put the baby on the open oven door to "thaw him out," for he was blue with cold soon after leaving the womb. The children, who had been sent to the mailbox, were begging to be let into the house, but the baby had not arrived. Ma recalled seeing the noses pressed against the window and the eyes peering through holes scraped clear in the frost and ice on the windows, for Pa would not let the children in from the cold until Dick was safely in this world.

Shortly after Dick's birth, the family settled on a ranch much closer to town. That land is still farmed today by children of my oldest brother, Tot. It was here that I was born, and I don't know where Pa sent the other children, since our mailbox was just a few hundred yards from the house.

It seems remarkable that Ma had no miscarriages, no

Mika, holding Dick, with
Gene, about 1930
(Asai family collection)

hemorrhages, no tearing of the tissues through eight deliveries. This says something about the style of life, the state of a woman's nervous system in those days, and Ma's mental health. She said she never suffered any pain or discomfort after any of the deliveries. This contrasts with all the pain and difficulties I experienced with the birth of my first son, no thanks to the "help" of an obstetrician. I still have lingering resentment toward that doctor who caused permanent damage to my bladder.

The first time Ma went to see a doctor was between her first few births. He told her she was pregnant. She scoffed, "Ridiculous! I should know when I'm pregnant, and I'm not pregnant." The doctor was shocked to learn that she had never drunk milk in her life and ordered her to get milk to drink daily. She ordered milk from a neighbor who had a milk cow and tried to drink it.

She remarked that the first few years she lived in America, the most repulsive thing to her was the smell of an American home with its odor of milk, cheese, butter, and all the dairy products. It overwhelmed her when she stepped into American homes, which brought on a wave of nausea. She added that she wondered if Caucasians had the same reaction when they came to Japanese homes with the smell of soy sauce, fish, and other Japanese odors. In later years, when we traded fruit and vegetables to the Celilo Indians for salmon, I remember the strong smell of fish that permeated their huts and tents. There was much family discussion of that after every visit to Celilo Falls (which was later submerged by the Columbia River behind the Dalles Dam in 1957).

The milk diet did not last long, but Ma did not bother to tell the doctor so. As time went by, she noticed a large lump in her abdomen, which rolled from side to side as she turned in bed. Surgery was finally performed to remove a tumor that was so large it filled a washbasin. Baby, indeed!

Ma's aversion to milk products was partly due to prejudice, cultural unfamiliarity, and possibly lactose intolerance. When she was older and visited the grandchildren, she loved to bring Cheetos or some other cheese-like tidbits. She liked to eat them but would never buy them at home for herself. When I told her they were made of cheese, she didn't believe me at first. This happened not long before our second son, Kenneth, who vowed he hated tomatoes, learned that ketchup was made of tomatoes. He couldn't believe it.

Ma's experience with medical men was not positively reinforced with regard to dentists. By her late thirties, her teeth had deteriorated so much that she needed false teeth. A combination of diet and too many children probably contributed to the early loss of her teeth. (She had eaten little or no sweets or sugar, for the family diet was mostly Japanese, consisting of rice and fresh vegetables and fruit.) She went to town one day and had all her teeth pulled in a mass extraction, went home, and waited until false teeth could be made and fitted. It was a miserable, painful affair, as one might imagine. I never knew Ma when she had anything but store-bought teeth. She was 40 years old when I was born, the last of her eight children.

Because snow would fall as much as two or three feet during a night or day, Pa had to take the horse and sled and clear the road for the children to walk to Oak Grove Grade School, five miles away. He would never let the children ride, but instead made them run along behind the sled to keep warm. Although he bundled up, he said he sometimes nearly froze while sitting and guiding the horse. Others accused him of being cruel and heartless for not letting the children ride, but he was sure he was doing the right thing. All I know is that all of my brothers and remaining sister were blessed with good health and strong constitutions. Tot, Min, and Gene lived to age 85. Half died in a car accident at 29. Mika passed away in November 2022 at 99. Dick died at 64, and I am still going strong and coming up on 92 this year.

On one occasion, my sister Mika began to cry on her way to school, saying she was too cold to go any farther. Although her brothers tried to explain that she had already come three miles and there were only two more miles to reach the school, she turned around and ran home to warmth. Pa was well up ahead with the horse and sled, unaware he had lost Mika until she was long gone. When school let out in the afternoon, Pa was there, having cleared the fresh snow that had fallen during the day.

During those cold winters, Mika recalled that she sometimes stayed home a month or two and caught up with the class after she returned to school in the spring, when the weather warmed up. She proudly stated that she stayed with her grade throughout all those years, never falling behind despite winter absences. She also remembered that the homemade coat Ma had made for her to wear was too thin and cold to withstand the coldest temperatures of those months.

Along a good portion of the road to school was a large irrigation ditch, too wide to jump across and deep enough to drown several people over the years. Anything that fell into Ditch Creek was as good as lost forever. My brother Min got a new cap for the first day of school, only to lose it the same day in a cap-tossing adventure with his playmates on the way home. It must have cost a few precious pennies or dollars, because Ma told the story many times, and each time she did, she had the same sad expression on her face. It may have been the same expression she had on her face the day the cap was lost, when she learned that it now sat at the bottom of Ditch Creek. She would have preferred it to be on Min's head.

Since my parents knew none of the traditions and holidays of their adopted country, the children had to learn about them through experience. Mika said her first year at school she only received valentines on Valentine's Day. The following year she knew enough to give some! For the first four or five years of my life, I had no calls from Santa Claus at Christmas, and not because I hadn't been a good girl. Someone had forgotten to tell my parents about him.

The only exception to this was a life-sized doll I received from my parents when I was 4 or 5 years old. Everyone said it was as large as I was. I still have that doll in my possession. It has the old plaster face that all dolls had then. They warned me not to let the doll get exposed to bright sunshine, for fear that her complexion would "crack." I often pushed it in a doll buggy with its hat pulled over its face, but today it bears many cracks on its cheeks.

Since Mika was nine years older than I, she was able to play Santa Claus for a few years. When she had me hang my stocking behind our wood stove, Pa laughed and asked me if I thought a fat Santa could squeeze himself down our skinny stovepipe, and what would he do if he could? He'd fall right into the hot coals of our fire.

Pa suggested that I borrow one of his large wool work socks, which was much larger than any sock I owned. I believed in Santa until 1941, when I was 9 years old and Pearl Harbor was attacked.

Pa at Timberline on Mount Hood with Dick, a friend, and Gene at far right. Dick was about 5 or 6 here, and Gene 9. Note that the building is not the famed Timberline Lodge, which would not be built for several more years. This photo dates from about 1934. (Asai family collection)

Santa wrote me a note in my stocking, saying that Christmas would have to be a little slim this year because of the war and world situation. I recognized my sister's writing, and the illusion was over.

My mother couldn't really write at all—not even in Japanese, much less English—so instead of a signature, she made an X on the back of her Social Security checks to cash them. When I was a junior or senior in high school and she was in her fifties, I tried to teach my mother how to sign her name. Eventually she was able to sign in English letters, except that cursive letters are rounded, and Japanese words are rendered in strokes. They're only horizontal, vertical, or dots. So my mother's signature had a funny, angular quality to it. Her M's had roofs on them. And circular A's were difficult for her.

We children spoke English to each other. But only when we were sassy and disrespectful did we speak to Pa and Ma in English. In this way, we were all bilingual from an early age. Only the eldest, Tot, was held back in the first grade because of his difficulty with the English language. He had had no siblings to speak English with before he entered school. The first year of school was for the purpose of learning the English language. It was quite a common thing for the eldest child of a Japanese family to be held back in the first grade, as Tot was. The rest of us benefited from our older brothers and sisters.

My parents valued education above all things and made family sacrifices to help us succeed academically. Perhaps this is because Ma had a two-grade education and Pa a six-grade one, obtained with some degree of hardship in Japan, where most of Pa's peers got no more than two or three years of schooling.

Half graduated from the eighth grade in about 1932, during the Great Depression. My parents leased the use of another orchard to plant and harvest strawberries. This was done in an orchard of young trees that were not yet bearing fruit. The full net profit from the strawberry crop went toward the purchase of a wool suit for Half's elementary school graduation. Wool in those days was not what it is now. It had to be handled with care, and shrinkage was a great problem. The trousers were "knickers," or knee pants with cuffs that buttoned. The suit had a matching cap.

On the first day of school the following autumn, Half wore this suit to town as a freshman in high school. As part of traditional hazing of freshmen, new students were thrown into the watering trough in front of the school. When Half came home from school that day, the sleeves of the suit reached only to his elbows, the knee pants were tight enough to cut off circulation in his legs, and the cap barely stayed on top of his head. Ma did not know whether to laugh or cry. All she could say was, "The whole strawberry crop."

In spite of the Depression, two of my brothers were sent to college in the late 1930s. Tot went to Oregon State College for two or three years to study agriculture. I was a preschooler then and can recall how happy I was to see him come home for vacation and for the summer. Min started at Linfield College on a chemistry scholarship and later transferred to Oregon State College for a year. But neither of my brothers was able to graduate, as my father could not afford to send them to four years of college in the Depression era. It was amazing that my father was able and so motivated to give education such a priority.

When Mika was 10 or 11 years old, Pa said she must cook breakfast for the family. There were nine of us in the family then. She fried potatoes and pancakes for breakfast almost every day. That meant she had to peel quite a few potatoes the night before, after washing all the supper dishes. Fried potatoes are still a favorite breakfast dish among many of the members of my family. My own sons love them and always remarked on how nice it was to visit Uncle Gene at his home in Albany, Oregon, because he often made fried potatoes for breakfast.

The Asai boys not only had to work in the orchard after school, but they also often had to run the tractor a couple of hours before breakfast and departure for school. Tot said he'd sometimes get on the school bus hot, sweaty, and un-showered after working in the morning. I am sure more than one brother tried to get out of this work repeatedly, but I remember the stories about Half the best.

Sometimes he would come home from school, grab his fishing pole, and sneak off with his friend, Harry Takagi, to go fishing. Knowing he would be in the doghouse for this escape, he would not come home until after dark. My parents seldom locked the door at night, but on these occasions they did, so Half would have to gain admittance. Ma recalled that in the silence of the night, she could hear Mika creep down the stairs to let Half in quietly. She also knew Mika had saved some of her supper to give to her brother. It was a secret between her and Half—and Ma. Nothing was ever said by Ma, Pa, Mika, or Half afterward. I think that Ma and Pa looked upon these incidents as natural and understandable behavior on the part of normal children.

One time Half was afraid to come home and face Pa and Ma, so he hid and slept in the attic of our "stone house," an aboveground storage building next to the house, used like a root cellar. There was sawdust up there, so it was a warm, dry place to sleep. I too often played in the stone house during my childhood. Half stayed there a couple days or more. Mika sneaked food to him: carrots, crackers, and such.

Mika believed that the reason Half was so often in trouble with our parents is that he was small for his age, younger than Tot and Min, yet expected to put in as much work as they. Having skipped two grades in school, he was even younger than perhaps my parents took into consideration. His friend Harry Takagi was a neighbor of the same age, but he was not required to work the way Half was.

When their first grandchildren in America were being born in the 1940s and 1950s, it was embarrassing to Ma when Pa would say to the son- or daughter-in-law in question, "Do you have plenty of hot water ready?" or "Have you saved plenty of rags?" Hospital births somehow lacked the excitement of childbirth as Pa and Ma experienced it.

Me with my parents outside the stone storage shed next to our house, October 24, 1935 (Asai family collection)

Pa said that by the time I came along, he had developed a good deal of confidence and self-assurance in delivering babies, having delivered seven of his own, plus a few others for his friends. It was only because of complications that he was unable to complete the job of delivering me. He was not mentally prepared for the challenge that presented itself: I entered the world with one arm and one leg. There I stopped.

Ma was caught in the hardest moments of labor and delivery for several hours. She was not in the habit of complaining at any time in her life, not even during the previous seven deliveries. Pa said she would simply grasp the metal frame of her bedstead till her fingers turned white. He would wipe her face again and again as she perspired profusely, but she never uttered a word.

With this eighth baby, though, she burst out in a tirade such as Pa had never heard before. "Kill the baby or do something!" she cried. "I have seven healthy children; one more does not matter, but do something!" Pa was frantic. Should he leave her alone? Should he go to town and seek out Dr. Chick? The baby wouldn't budge, and Ma was suffering terribly, so Pa hitched up the horse and rode several miles into town. He returned finally with Dr. Chick and his nurse. Ma was still alive and suffering. The doctor poked his arm in, turned the baby around, and out into the world I popped.

The birth struggle had been so long and arduous that my body was red and swollen all over. Dr. Chick held me up by the heels and said, "Oh, a big boy!" His nurse frowned and poked him. "What do you mean? Look again." Pa seemed to enjoy the embarrassment I felt as he retold this story when I was old enough to understand. Ma remarked on the great discomfort she felt when Dr. Chick reached in to turn the baby. When my first son was born, the obstetrician reached in to seize the baby with forceps, and the memory of my mother's words came back to me in a rush.

As if that were not enough suffering for Ma, I was the only baby she did not nurse for a full two years, because I bit her nipples bloody with my early-appearing teeth. She also said that I had boils or eczema on my face and head as an infant, and because I would scratch myself bloody, she tied "gloves" over my hands. When that did not prevent the scratching, she tied my hands behind my back and put me to sleep on my tummy. She hated to do it, but she had to work while Mika tended me, as I wailed continually, unhappy to lose the free movement of my arms. Perhaps my habit of talking with many hand and arm movements is an attempt to make up for those early months of confinement.

We were never watched during the workday except by older brothers and sisters, or as we grew old enough to toddle about in the orchard near where my parents were working. Ma said Pa constructed a sort of playpen. She would clean up the breakfast dishes, sweep the floor, get the baby fed and settled for the day, put him in the playpen unattended, and go out and work. Once or twice during the morning she would go home and change the baby's pants or simply peek in the window then leave again. The same procedure was followed in the afternoon.

Seldom did she find the child crying, distraught, or seeming to be lonely. More often he was sleeping, goo-gooing, and/or entertaining himself happily. Ma observed the births and rearing of her many grandchildren with amazement. She wondered how all her children could have survived and enjoyed such good health with a minimum of broken bones, burns, falls, and the like. Modern babies seemed so protected and pampered and restrained at every turn. She never had vitamin drops or cow's milk to give us, and very little meat. (This may have been a fortunate happenstance for us.)

Ma was puzzled as to why her grandchildren and all other modern babies seemed less able to cope alone and be happy, and why they needed so much time and attention. She felt that genuine interest in the child when the parents were present gave the child a feeling of being wanted, and that should sustain him or her during times the parents were away. She could not believe that children today could be so different from her own children. She remarked that fears modern mothers expressed about all the things that *could* happen to a child alone probably *did* happen to her children, except she did not know about them. Somehow they survived. She likewise did not expend any anxieties or fears prior to their happening.

I am convinced that fears and loneliness are taught to children by parents who may subconsciously desire a certain level of dependency from them. In the rearing of our own children, Don and I put these ideas to work, and the results confirmed to us the possible value of our beliefs.

In 1950, when Half died in an automobile accident, Pa turned to Ma and inquired, "Why didn't we have more children?" Ma simply answered, "That's all we could have." When I had my second child in the 1960s and Ma came to Eugene to help me, I found to my surprise that she did not know that most women cannot conceive while nursing a baby. She mused aloud to me about the mystery of why all her children were spaced two and a half to three years apart, when in fact she did not practice any birth control. The fact that she nursed almost all of her children for two years had not connected to the spacing of her children, in her mind. When I suggested this notion, she was as surprised as I, that she had not heard this before.

Aside from the attendance of a doctor at my complicated birth, Ma had no further encounters with physicians except for necessary surgery, which came at least twice more before she was through with them all. I tried to attribute eight "operations" to my mother's life—one for each of the babies she had—a notion commonly held by children before they learn the details about the facts of life. That mistaken idea was straightened out in my mind when I entered adolescence in the Heart Mountain Relocation Center in Wyoming during World War II.

People have said about my mother: She gave birth to all those children, she stayed home and she made your clothes, she cooked, she cleaned house, she did the laundry, and then she worked ten or twelve hours out in the orchard . . . she must have been miserable! And I said no, she was happy because she was the most successful person around. In order to be a good wife and a good mother, she had to do these things, and she did them all. So she was a complete success. Sometimes, it's not what we do or think or say—it's how we live.

The family in the snow (left to right): Gene, me with my beloved doll, Half behind Ma and Pa, Dick, and Mika in 1937 (Asai family collection)

CHAPTER 5

Family Life and Training

When I was in the third and fourth grades, in accord with my parents' training schedule, I was expected to learn to cook. Although my sister Mika, who was nine years older than I, and my mother were both at home, I was given the responsibility of cooking the evening meal every day, usually for eight or nine people. Mika graduated from high school in 1941, when I was 9 years old, and got a live-in job keeping house and helping the Sche family (pronounced "Shay"), who lived in town and had a jewelry store. After Mika's graduation, she was gone most days of the summer and most of the fall until the attack on Pearl Harbor.

How well I remember coming home from school to an empty house, where the only sounds were those of the flies and bees buzzing about the living-dining room and kitchen. All the family was working out in the orchard. There was a note on the table from Ma (written in haste during a short lunch hour) giving me further instructions she might have forgotten to deliver orally in the morning before I left for school and reminding me of the important points. These instructions were written in her elementary school Japanese syllabary, which was all she had learned in the two years of formal schooling she received before she stayed home to work in the rice paddies.

I could read the simple Japanese syllabary of my mother's notes because Pa had seen to it that all the children learned to read and write the two syllabaries, *kata kana* and *hiragana*. We used to play Japanese card games (*karuta*) during the long winter nights. The games were designed to teach us the syllabaries. Pa gave each of us a caramel or piece of candy at the end of the game, and an extra piece went to the winner—the one who got the most right. This served as an incentive to learn the syllabary well. Simple things motivated children in those days.

I changed out of my school clothes, a habit my mother required of us all from an early age, and then carried in wood to fill the box next to the wood cookstove. Sometimes the evening meal would require that I go to the garden to gather or pick vegetables. Corn on the cob was a great favorite in the family, and Pa regularly planted three crops of corn, in staggered fashion, so that a new one was ready to harvest when we had eaten the preceding crop. Ma used to take a head count of the number of ears each person wanted to eat. Then she'd try to find that many ears in the garden. They would have to be cooked in a wash boiler to accommodate the large number of ears.

When the family came home for dinner, the corn would be ready to eat. We all sat on the back porch and ate several ears apiece as an appetizer for the meal. Sometimes someone would complain of being short an ear because someone else might have eaten more ears than he had ordered. There was always a little playful arguing about that. We'd throw the cobs out in the orchard in front of the house for the chickens to pick at, and then we would go into the house for supper.

We had a separate building for our Japanese bath: a large, deep tub built of sheet metal over an open fire that heated the bath water. At five o'clock, I began the ritual of cooking supper and readying the bath, which required running back and forth from the kitchen to the bathhouse to tend the two wood fires. Trying to keep the temperatures controlled somehow so the bath water would be warm enough yet not too hot, and the rice and vegetables would not overcook, was not easy for a third grader.

For a Japanese bath, a person dips water out of the tub into a small basin or pan. After dousing himself and soaping and rinsing several times (a drain in the concrete or tile floor takes all the splashed water out through the floor), the person, now clean, climbs into the big tub and sits and soaks in water deep enough to come up to his chin. If the bath water temperature is perfectly achieved, there is enough water for each person to dip his washing water out and still leave enough in the tub for a deep soak. If the water is too hot, so much cold water has to be added that the tub overflows. If the water is not warm enough, so much is dipped out by the succession of bathers that the water level is too low for the later bathers to soak in deep water.

At such times, we would have to relight the fire to bring the temperature back up to a comfortable level. On such occasions, the bathhouse would sometimes get so smoky that we sat in the tub with our eyes watering. An added discomfort was the fire's heat on our bare bottoms as we sat on the raft made of wooden slats, which we submerged in the tub as protection from the sheet-metal lining.

Steaming rice to perfection, cooking vegetables to the crisp textures demanded by Japanese tastes, and achieving the perfect water temperature and water level were all easier said than done.

Ma was able to accomplish all these tasks to a standard of perfection the family had come to expect. Pa and my brothers were typical Japanese men when it came to expressing what they thought and how they felt. Every evening I heard, "The rice is too dry" or "The rice is soggy"; "The bath was too hot—I had to overflow it"; "The beans are too salty" or "The asparagus is overcooked."

Sometimes I would even try to make dessert. The oven temperature was hard to keep constant on the wood stove, and baked goods often came out lighter or darker than hoped for. My offerings were received with, "Are these brownies or blackies? Are these biscuits or rocks?" Sometimes my productions were bounced on the table.

Tears were a regular experience on my part—tears I hid in the kitchen or in my room. If none of the family was aware of my tears, I am certain Ma always was. Yet she never rescued me with a "Come on, boys, she's only learning to cook," or a "Pa, she's only 8 years old," or a "That's all right, honey."

All my life she and Pa let me (and all the children) earn successes and failures, savoring or suffering them alone. I would later learn that this was the most difficult thing to do as a mother and a teacher myself. As I watched my peers and their families, I was glad not to be shown off, bragged about, or, conversely, blamed, chastised, nagged, disowned—all those things that rob a child of self-respect, self-reliance, pride, independence, and above all, a balanced sense of self-evaluation.

Whenever I did anything good in my mind, my parents didn't praise me. Likewise, if I did something I was not proud of, they wouldn't say, "Why did you do that? That was terrible." Nothing was ever said, but because of the pride and respect they developed in us, we wanted to do what would make them proud and feel good about us. At the same time, if we did something that we could not feel proud of ourselves, they didn't scold us or punish us for it. We came to enjoy our successes and regret our failures all by ourselves.

With each failure, I found myself running over in my mind the instructions and details Ma had given me, and finding for myself where I had erred and how I could improve. One learns quickly in the school of hard knocks, and knocks came hard and often from the six male members of the household. If I could not find my mistake on my own, I would ask Ma for help. She never volunteered the help first, so I had a chance to depend on my own resources, but I knew I would not be left without support if I needed it. It was a matter of pride that I did not call on her until I had exhausted my own resources first.

Ma was always there, and it is characteristic of her that although she was aware of my daily tears and suffering over the cooking experience, she forgot about them as the years went by. When I was in my thirties and she was in her seventies, I recounted the experience of those years to her. To my surprise, she responded with tears, saying, "Did you really cry every night? Why, I had forgotten," and she wept anew at the thought of my having suffered so much over my nightly chore.

My cooking lessons were interrupted by the wartime years, but when our family returned to Hood River after a three-year interlude, I was in the seventh grade and resumed cooking suppers and helped with other meals from then until I left home for college in 1950. By this time the family had shrunk to only four to six persons around the table.

She never said a word, but a job that had to be done was either done by the one who was supposed to do it, or Ma would do it. She disliked having dirty dishes left after any meal for more than a half hour, and it was expected that I should also wash the dishes when the meal was over. Not only was the job necessary, but the proper time to do it was just as important.

Sometimes I would shirk that duty, and if a half hour passed, Ma would quietly get up and do the dishes, which made me feel so ashamed that I seldom sat down after the meal again. I felt worse about her doing it than doing it myself. This went for wiping off the dinner table, kitchen drainboard, and stove; habits I hold to this day. I find that my tolerance for a dirty table, dirty counters, and a sink full of dirty dishes is very low.

This strict attention to the simple tasks of everyday living (sweeping the floor, making the beds, hanging up every piece of clothing taken off, etc.) helped me immensely when I left home.

The habits were well formed. My college roommates all remarked that I moved like a robot—jumping out of bed at the first ring of the alarm, mending or ironing and setting out my clothes the night before wearing, brushing my teeth, making my bed—but I noticed that I got a great deal more done by eight o'clock than anyone else around, and I was never in a spot of having nothing but dirty socks or a tear in my dress when I needed to wear those items. I sensed that my roommates, while laughing at my rigid attention to personal and household matters, envied the training I had received at home.

When my brother Gene came home on furlough one holiday, I was in the kitchen with a mountain of dirty dishes after a huge holiday feast we had enjoyed. He pushed me out and declared that he was going to do the dishes this time. He had done KP duty in the army many times and now realized what it had been like for me all those years in the kitchen, cooking for the family and washing all the dishes too. Any injustice or bitterness I had felt all those years floated away in a single meal's dishwashing.

Because I realized that I would be cooking for myself in later years, I decided I should learn some favorite family recipes from my mother. Ma sometimes baked what we called Mt. Hood cupcakes. They rose in the middle and were shaped like Mt. Hood, which we could see from our kitchen window. We had few sweets or desserts, and anything that had any sweetness

Me in coveralls on the farm, age 5 or 6 (Asai family collection)

to it was a special treat. These were not really cupcakes, which are even sweeter, but more like what I later learned are muffins.

I asked Ma how to mix up a batch of Mt. Hood cupcakes. She told me she used a certain tin cup, which had a dent in it. She measured flour up to the dent and used two such "dent" measures. I protested that I didn't have such a cup. Her reply was, "Well, I can't help that. That's your problem," and she laughed. She also explained the reason they were peaked in the middle was because of the heat in the oven of our wood stove. She wasn't sure I could achieve the same shape of cupcake in another stove's oven. She was right: I have never been able to make the Mt. Hood cupcakes I loved so much.

On another occasion, she taught me how to wash and measure rice for steaming. She said that after rinsing the rice a few times and running the water off, I should fill the pot with water above the rice, measuring to the joints of my fingers as I stood my hand vertically in the pot, with the tips of my fingers touching the bottom. I protested that my fingers were longer than hers. She said, "I can't help that, and it doesn't make any difference." That did not make sense to me. For years I did not trust this method, so I carefully measured one part rice, one part water.

Years later, when my sister came to visit me in my home in Coos Bay, Oregon, Mika asked if she could help me with the dinner preparations by washing the rice. I told her to go ahead. I noticed that she placed her hand vertically in the rice pot, to measure the water up to the joints of her fingers! I asked if she had always done that to cook rice, and she said, "Why, yes. Don't you?"

My turn to teach Ma something came in 1950, the year that my eldest brother Tot got married. In anticipation of having his wife take over the cooking duties of the household, he bought an electric range. Ma could not read the directions for use or the control switches on the new stove, so I had to teach her. The job was made somewhat easier by the fact that we got a model that had different-colored push buttons for the various temperatures (red for high, blue for medium high, etc.).

In the years before I was old enough to know about my brothers' and sister's experiences, a few stories stand out in my memory as though I had experienced them myself. Since the Issei (first-generation Japanese) seldom got together, they had much socializing to do when they did gather in a public place, such as at a school function. They would congregate and talk loudly in Japanese. Mika admitted that she felt ashamed of our parents and hid at school programs and graduations when Pa and Ma attended them.

I had the same feelings in the postwar years, when anti-Japanese feeling was high. If Ma went to stores in town with me (a rare occasion), I would whisper to her in the hope that she would likewise whisper to me, rather than speak out loud to my embarrassment. When my school friends came over to play and my parents spoke Japanese to me, I answered in English. This was rude behavior toward my parents, but in those years I was more interested in peer acceptance than in showing my parents respect.

Pa kept important business papers, sales receipts, bills, and other documents poked onto a piece of baling wire attached to a nail in the kitchen (a kind of makeshift spindle). Once when Pa and Ma were working in the orchard, my brother Min lit those papers on fire. When Ma came home at noon to make lunch, she saw smoke pouring out of the house; thankfully, no one was inside. She was able to put out the fire easily, and little damage was done to the house.

Imagine the fright it gave them, not to mention my father's chagrin at losing all his business papers. This must have occurred in the 1930s, because it happened in the home where I was born in 1932. Ma never mentioned any threat to human life, which means I must have been old enough to be out in the orchard with my parents. Brother Min would have been in his teens, which was a little old to be playing with matches. Pa suspected that he was "rolling his own" with Pa's business papers, a poor substitute for cigarette paper, for all concerned.

Brother Half was 15 when he graduated from high school in 1935. He was the third son and fourth child. He had skipped two grades. Mika said he was so short that his feet did not touch the floor as he sat on stage at the graduation ceremonies. Shortly after graduation, Half took a job working on the railroad about eight miles from home. He lived in cabins along with the other railroad section gang employees (as Pa had done while a young bachelor fresh from Japan two decades before) and came home most weekends. With his earnings, he had his badly neglected teeth fixed.

Half had a love for music that had not been fully satisfied, and as the years went by, he would come home, "hole up" in his room, and practice various musical instruments he bought for himself. Harmonica, guitar, clarinet, and saxophone were the ones I saw. When he was gone to work during the week and no one else was around, I would sneak into his room and blow a few notes on his instruments, unaware that I was destined to marry a professional musician and music teacher twenty years later.

In the late 1930s, my parents purchased a piano from a door-to-door salesman who hauled pianos on a truck and made home sales. Mika took piano lessons. She often accompanied Min, who liked to sing. "Give Me My Boots and Saddle" and "My Buddy" were a couple of his favorites. This same piano was used by Tot's family for piano lessons for all four of his children. Today it sits in the Hood River home of Tot's eldest daughter, Marta Cannell, on an orchard not far from the "home place." It is the piano pictured with Ma and Pa in a feature story that ran in the *Oregonian* after the war (see photo on page 141).

CHAPTER 6

Father as Zen

True Zen Buddhists are vegetarians. They have a reverence for life similar to the beliefs of Albert Schweitzer. Although Pa ate meat until his death, he apparently had some misgivings about it. I remember him saying, "Ameri-ken eat too much meat" and urging us to be moderate in our meat-eating. He attributed the prevalent illnesses in the Western world (heart disease and cancer in particular) to excess consumption of meat and dairy products. Modern-day dieticians have expressed similar ideas.

We kept chickens most of the years I was growing up, both before and after World War II. My mother never killed the chickens, which were served for our Sunday dinners. When Pa chopped off a chicken's head, I was usually with him: to pick up the flopping chicken, put it in a bucket, and carry it home to douse it in hot water for defeathering, which was my special job. He would lay the chicken's head on the chopping block and repeat over and over, *Namu Amida Butsu, Namu Amida Butsu,* a kind of Buddhist rosary. (Amida Butsu refers to Lord Buddha.)

I thought this was a half-joking gesture, a kind of prayer for the chicken's soul, soon to ascend to heaven. Much later in life, I realized that the prayer was for Pa's own soul—for taking the chicken's life. After World War II, he had no more to do with killing the

Sunday chicken; he had lost heart for it. He was in his sixties by this time. Pa had too many chicken murders on his hands already. Thenceforth Ma killed them, with as little joy as my father had experienced all those years.

Pa used to say that guilt and grudges held against fellow human beings form knots inside a person, knots that would eventually kill him. The safe thing was to do nothing in this life to cause guilt and to let others' wrongdoing pass by, washing away out of mind and heart.

Although he took his Buddhist faith and practice seriously, he never imposed it on any of us children, as some other Japanese Buddhist parents did. He felt, however, that a religious faith was important and wanted his children to find it in some form. He believed that all the religions of the world had a common code of ethics and spirit of brotherhood and morality important to all humans. For us, his children, he believed Christianity was the "right" religion, consonant with the culture we were living in. Although he never verbalized this, I think he thought that for us to be Buddhists in America would mean we'd be cultural misfits.

The family in 1938 or '39: Tot, me, Dick, and Gene surround Ma and Pa (Asai family collection)

I had heard that even before I was born, in the 1920s and '30s, Pa would drive a carload of young people to Portland to see the Passion Play at Eastertime. At least two of my brothers remembered being included in that carload. Portland was a seventy-three-mile trip on the winding Columbia River Highway (now known as the Scenic Columbia River Highway), which loops around and around up to Crown Point and down to Portland.[1] In a Model T or Model A, the hilly and curving trip would take three to four hours, whereas today it's barely sixty miles straight down the Columbia Gorge on Interstate 84 and takes less than one hour.

As his family grew, Pa encouraged all of us to go to Sunday school. There was a Japanese Methodist Church in Hood River, which met in the Japanese Community Hall. My sister remained active in the Methodist Church all her life. Years before the war, photographs show the hall with American and Japanese flags standing on either side of the entrance out front. Back then, it wouldn't have been inflammatory to see a Japanese flag in Hood River. Reverend Isaac Inouye was the minister there for years. He also taught Japanese-language classes on Saturday. Christian or not, Pa treated Rev. Inouye with the greatest respect, for respect was due anyone with knowledge and education. I believe Rev. Inouye was a graduate of Oberlin College, so he was well educated as well as bilingual.

The weekends meant a trip to the Japanese Hall for language school on Saturday and Sunday school on Sunday. My brothers referred to those as royal days of cops and robbers, hide and seek, and prison ball; the amount of language learning or religious training may have been pitifully small.

Pa was a leader and respected member of the Japanese community in Hood River. In a letter after the Second World War, Masuo Yasui, an Issei immigrant of Pa's generation who owned a general store downtown (and about whose family we'll hear more later), addressed my father as "big brother Asai."[2] As far back as I can remember, Pa received regular visits from other Japanese heads of households or couples, who came to obtain his opinion or advice on matters of all kinds, be it a choice of marriage partner for their children, a farm or business investment, a domestic quarrel between spouses or parents and children, or a decision to be made by the Japanese community. The seriousness or private nature of the subject could be gauged by whether we children were sent out of the room.

In the years after 1945, when our family returned to Hood River after being kept in government prison camps for three years and our reception was less than friendly, I went to the Valley Christian Church alone every Sunday morning and evening. I can't remember whether Pa suggested I do so or if I decided to go on my own; I think the latter was the case. Before the war, I was too young to go alone to the Japanese Methodist Church in town (five miles away) or to the Japanese-language school with my brothers and sister. That means I did not attend the Valley Christian Church either.

At any rate, I believe it was my own decision to go to church. My family did not discourage me from it, nor did they encourage it or provide transportation. Since the church was more than a mile from my home, I was able to walk there, which I did twice on Sundays. Sundays were often workdays on the farm, just the same as weekdays. For me, going to church was possibly motivated in part by a desire to get a day of rest from work on the farm.

Even though no one would sit in the same pew with me or speak to me in Sunday school and church after the war, Pa still felt the church was doing both of us a service in the matter of moral and spiritual teaching for me. He felt a responsibility for this and would make a fifty-dollar contribution to the church now and then. In spirit, it was akin to paying for music lessons, but the pastor never fully understood this and began to make house calls to encourage my parents to join the church or at least to attend the

Sunday services. Pa must have been a little amused by the visits, but he never showed any such thought to anyone.

Every morning and sometimes in the evening, Pa would sit in front of the Buddhist worship altar in his bedroom (a small miniature closet affair, set atop his dresser or chest of drawers), light incense, hit his ceremonial gong, and drone out his religious chant for the day. I can hear the same tune of the chant even today, in my mind's ear. I attended Buddhist services a few times in later years and felt very much at home when I heard the familiar tune that I had heard coming from Pa's bedroom.

In my first two years of college, I began to think in depth about Pa's ideas and attitudes concerning religion. It didn't make sense to me. When schoolmates learned that my parents were Buddhists, they asked me to tell them about Buddhism. Once while home from college on vacation, I questioned him about his broadmindedness. I asked him why, as a Buddhist, he had not instructed us in the precepts of his faith. Pa did his best to explain. With the language barrier, it was difficult to communicate, especially on such topics as religion, philosophy, values, and moral issues. He could not express himself well enough in English, and my knowledge of Japanese did not extend much beyond the level of "Please pass the sugar" and "I don't feel like it."

He said something like, "I was born in Japan and grew up there. I was brought up as a Buddhist in a Buddhist family and a Buddhist culture. In my life, when I do something, I cannot tell you whether I do it because I am Japanese or because I'm Buddhist. Japan is a very old culture and Buddhism is a very old religion, as compared to the United States and Christianity, both of which are very young. Japanese culture and Buddhism are completely intertwined, but American culture and Christianity are very separate. Just look around you. What does the Bible teach, and what do people do on Sunday as compared to what they do daily in their businesses and in the work world? I have read the Bible and find there a wealth of good teaching. Just study it and try to live according to its teaching so that one day, perhaps, Christianity will become so much a part of you in practice that you will not be able to distinguish it from your cultural practices. Then, perhaps you will be able to understand what I am trying to tell you."

I did not understand the depth of his wisdom and understanding at the time, but his words have stayed with me since then, and I have puzzled over their full meaning many times. Sometimes I think I know what he was trying to say to me.

About five or six years after this conversation, I got a hint of his philosophy when I visited my cousins in Japan. During my Fulbright year there, I lived in Shizuoka Prefecture, the "Florida of Japan," where tangerines and oranges grow in abundance. Before I left Shizuoka to visit my uncle's house, I sent a crate of fruit to be given to his family and to be shared with other relatives' households in Aichi and Mie Prefectures. When I arrived at my uncle's house, I saw that they had received the fruit some days earlier but had not opened the crate, waiting instead for my arrival. The crate was opened before my eyes, and the women of the three households to share the fruit got down on their knees on the hardened dirt floor in the entrance to my uncle's house to divide the oranges equally. They picked out all the largest ones first and divided those; then they did the same with the mediums and the smalls.

A small child, a granddaughter of one of the women, asked, "Are you through sorting now?" When her grandmother nodded, she grabbed the largest one and ran off with it. I thought to myself, "Children are the same the world over; she wants the largest one for herself." But I was wrong. She took that orange and placed it on the worship altar, where the first offerings of anything good to eat are always placed. This act was just as natural to her and her family as making the bed—an automatic thing.

In Pa's conversation with me, he added a warning. "If you try to take my culture or my religion away from me, you will kill one or both. So you can go to church, study the Bible, and practice your faith all you want, but don't preach to me . . . even though the Bible does instruct you to 'Go and preach to all nations.'" Live and let live was carried out to a beautiful degree in his life. When I read books on Zen many years later, I could look back and recall seeing Zen in practice in the daily life of my father over all those years. I just did not recognize or appreciate its beauty at the time.

My experience with Mrs. Steele, my first- and second-grade teacher before the war, provides a stark illustration of my father's philosophy in action. Before the war, I had been the teacher's pet and enjoyed special attention and many favors from her. When we returned home from the camps in 1945, I was in the seventh grade. I had had no direct communication with Mrs. Steele since our return, but I did pass by her husband's business, the Rockford Store, a mile from my house, every day on my way to and from school. Only now there was a "No Jap Trade" sign hanging in the window.

On several occasions after our return to Hood River, I saw Mrs. Steele and tried to speak to her. Each time she either turned or walked away from me, out of shame or embarrassment, I am sure, rather than hate or dislike. Once I stood in line at the bank, and she was the next in line, so I looked and smiled at her, and she didn't even wait to get her business done at the bank. She just left. So it was a surprise to me when I began to see my name in the neighborhood news column of the local newspaper written by Mrs. Steele. How did this come about?

Our little local newspaper, the *Hood River News*, carried a kind of gossip column that was written by Mrs. Steele after she was dismissed by the school principal for some kind of infraction. Mrs. Porter, the pastor's wife who was sympathetic to me, would send Mrs. Steele church and church-related news to include in her column. I had been elected president of the church youth fellowship, even in the face of not being fully accepted by the congregation or socially included by the youth group members, and that was mentioned. After I graduated from high school and went on to college, Mrs. Porter would tell of my visits home on school vacations, which Mrs. Steele would report in her column. Complimentary items like "Mitzi Asai is home visiting her parents on college vacation" would turn up, which was surprising to me, and really kind of amusing.

One time I sat down with Pa to ask his opinion of Mrs. Steele and how I should deal with her. I asked if I should go to her house and make overtures of friendship, in the privacy of her home and out of the public eye. Pa gave me this reply: "I have read the Bible and have studied the teachings of Christianity. I know that you are taught to turn the other cheek and to walk the second mile, and that you must forgive those who have wronged you. Although I can see some merit in such teachings, as a Buddhist and as a person brought up in Japanese culture, I must look at the situation from a different perspective. I believe that each person must build his own character through personal will and action. When a person (in this case, you) helps someone else work on building that person's character, that person's strength of character has been diluted, as opposed to the case of each individual's being responsible for the building of his own.

"In Mrs. Steele's case, I perceive that she has done wrong to you and to us. To go to her and be friendly and even to forgive without her bringing up the subject of her behavior is to rob her of the opportunity of doing something about it herself, unaided and unabetted. If you make it easier for her, she can never feel the pride in herself were she to make the first move to rectify her past actions. There would always be a small element of shame or weakness recognized by her. Therefore, you would be doing her a disservice. I would not go to her home."

Those seemed like harsh words to me at the time, but as the years go by, I can better understand the wisdom of them. Mrs. Steele died the year I was in Japan teaching English on the Fulbright program, so I never had a chance to change my mind. I shall never know what passed through her mind and heart.

Pa enjoyed good health all his life and was a model for his peers. After he reached 60, it was a common thing for someone to ask him what his formula for long life and good health was. He would reply that he worked hard every day, tried to do right by his fellow men, and when he laid his tired body down on a heavenly bed of comfort at night, he thanked God for the day and expressed his feeling that if he should die in the night, he would have died happily, satisfied with life. Then, as the morning sun crept into his room, he would say, "Thank God for another day to live!" I heard him say this many a day. This attitude toward life, he felt sure, contributed to his strength and good health.

CHAPTER 7

World War II

One weekend in June 1941, Half came home from his railroad job and asked Pa to sign a paper. He was going to volunteer in the US Army, he said. In those days, one had to be 21 to volunteer. You could be drafted at 20; otherwise, a parent's signature was required. Half was still 20 years old.

Pa demurred, so Half said he would forge Pa's signature if he didn't sign. Faced with this independent spirit, Pa signed the paper, and in June 1941, Half left for Ft. Lewis, Washington, and thence to Camp Roberts, California, for basic training. That lasted sixteen weeks. By the time his training was completed, he was nearly 21, for his birthday was in mid-September.

My brother was supposed to receive a furlough at this time, but it never materialized. In September, he wrote home to explain that all furloughs were postponed for a month, with no reasons given.

Half in US Army uniform (Asai family collection)

In October, he wrote to say that the furloughs had been postponed for a month a second time—again with no reasons given. In November, it was announced that all furloughs were canceled and all troops were to be moved to California to guard the coast.

My brother was sent to Santa Cruz. Why? To guard the coast against what? Although I was 9 years old at the time, I was old enough to surmise that someone, somewhere in our government and/or military, was expecting an attack. The draft had been going on for some time, and many boys had left Hood River for the armed forces.

On December 4, 1941, Tot was drafted, and he reported to the army induction center in Portland. So my oldest brother Tot, a draftee, and third-oldest brother, Half, a volunteer after he pressured Pa, entered the army before the United States officially entered World War II. Two more brothers, Min and Gene, would be drafted very late in the war, in 1944 or 1945.

Tot in US Army uniform
(Asai family collection)

About 5,000 Nisei (the Japanese term for the second generation, US citizens by birth) had been drafted before Pearl Harbor was attacked, but the attack caused the army to change its policy. Japanese American boys were reclassified by the Selective Service as "not acceptable to the armed forces due to nationality or ancestry" and were unwanted by draft boards.[1] Some already in uniform were discharged and sent home for no reason other than national origin. My two brothers were not sent home, however. Before the war was over, an estimated 33,300 Japanese Americans served in the armed forces, according to Selective Service figures.[2] About 20,000 served in the army like my brothers, and 800 were killed in action,[3] including my brother Half's friend Frank Hachiya.

On Friday, December 5, 1941, I went to school as usual and was treated the same as I always had been from the first day of the first grade at Barrett School in 1938. I had attended Barrett School for more than three years and been fully accepted. Little did I realize what the weekend's events would mean for me and my family over the next four years and more.

On Sunday, December 7, Pearl Harbor was attacked by the Japanese. How well I remember that day. I was playing at home when the news of the attack came over the radio. Pa was at the Hood River Japanese Community Hall that morning, where Rev. Inouye's Methodist Church, the language school, and social gatherings took place. Since 1926, when it was completed,[4] the Japanese community had used that facility for years without the benefit of a flush toilet; an outhouse located two or three hundred yards away from the hall served the purpose. The evening of December 7, 1941, was set for a fundraiser talent show, which they were hoping would raise enough money to install indoor plumbing. Pa and Mika, along with other Japanese people in the community, were industriously cleaning the hall in preparation for that evening's benefit event. I remember their excited return home, breathless and puzzled at being chased home by the sheriff and his deputies. They had been given no explanation for being sent away.

When we told Pa of the radio broadcast, the change in his expression indicated how clearly he understood what it all meant. Had Pa told the sheriff they were cleaning the hall for a talent show to raise money for an indoor toilet, it would have sounded ridiculous and unbelievable. Instead, the sheriff and his men assumed there was to be a great celebration of the attack on Pearl Harbor that night. The talent show was off, and the indoor toilet never became a reality. I understand the hall was sold after the war.

What it all meant for me became clear the next morning, when I returned to school. On Monday, I was in for a big surprise. I was spit upon twice and called "Jap," and some children refused to play with me at recess. I was hurt and bewildered. At 9 years old, in the fourth grade, I had never known discrimination before this moment. It was only a preview of the treatment I was to receive from grown-ups in Hood River four years later.

At the high school, the principal called a special meeting for the Japanese American students and told them to anticipate and expect some discrimination. The irony of my brother Half's being sent to Santa Cruz to guard the coast is that he was under the command of General DeWitt, the official who would largely be responsible for the mass removal of Japanese immigrants and Japanese Americans from the Pacific coastal states only a few months later.

Tot was at Ft. Lewis, Washington, on the day Pearl Harbor was attacked. The troops started camouflaging the fir trees on the base grounds, and at night there were blackouts. Although he did not experience any discrimination from other soldiers, he said he felt sorry for the few Blacks in his basic training group. The corporal and sergeant in the regular army were especially mean to the Black soldiers. They would not pass them the food in the mess halls, for example. "The Blacks just took it, said nothing, did nothing," Tot commented.

Right away, we were told that we were probably going to be taken out of our homes, so we should get ready. Min was home in Hood River. He said he had no fear of being removed from our homes or that anything would be done to us; we were US citizens, after all. But we knew by January that something was going to happen—we just didn't know what or when. When Executive

Order 9066 was announced in February 1942, it was a shock to my brother Min.

Instructions appeared in posters on telephone poles in many towns and cities where Japanese people lived, to tell them what they could expect to happen. The instructions included the phrase "both alien and non-alien." I didn't think anything about that in the fourth grade; even through high school and college it never occurred to me. But when I was in my fifties or so, I reread that and I thought, "Alien and non-alien"? I got very angry. All us kids were born in the United States, and our family happened to be from Oregon. We were American citizens. Why didn't they say "both alien and citizen"? Somebody, somewhere, knew what they were doing was not right and perhaps even unconstitutional, so they used seemingly specific yet evasive language.

A peculiar circumstance not understood by many Americans then or now is that my parents and their peers were not allowed to become American citizens before 1941, even though they had lived in the United States for more than thirty years.[5] Early laws passed in California and later in Washington and Oregon discriminated against Asians. Alien land laws were passed to prevent them from owning property. Naturalization laws barred Asians from the right of naturalization by omitting any reference to them.[6] My parents were therefore aliens and had to register themselves in their county seat of residence every year for decades. All of their children were Americans by reason of birth, however, having been born in the Hood River Valley.

It was not until 1952, when the US Supreme Court ruled such laws unconstitutional, and the McCarran-Walter Act passed, that my parents and their generation of Japanese were allowed to become naturalized US citizens. (Indian Americans and Filipino Americans had been accorded rights to naturalization in 1946 with the Luce-Celler Act.)[7] President Truman vetoed that bill not because he was opposed to it, but because it included quotas for potential allies that had domestic communist activity.[8] The bill was passed over Truman's veto. By then, Pa was 72 years old and Ma was 60. Pa felt that when he had wanted and needed citizenship the most, he could not have it. Now that it was available to him, he was too old and tired to try for it. My niece Tara says she recalls Pa studying for his exam, so perhaps he ran out of time or got distracted before he could take it.

I suspect he also feared that Ma might not be able to pass the citizenship test. Ma had had only a second-grade education in Japan, after which she quit in order to work the family farm. Pa's choosing her as his wife had rescued her from the rice paddies and brought her to an American fruit orchard. She could hardly read or write Japanese, much less enough English to pass a naturalization test—a test that would be challenging even for some natural-born American citizens. Without her, US citizenship would be empty indeed for him. I feel certain my parents would have had greater incentive to become more fluent in English if citizenship had been available to them sooner in their lives in America. As it was, they died in Oregon as Japanese citizens, after having lived here for more than fifty years.

Soon after Pearl Harbor, a curfew was imposed on all Japanese and people of Japanese descent in Hood River. Japanese aliens and citizens alike were to stay in their homes from eight o'clock in the evening to six o'clock the next morning. This curfew meant we were imprisoned in our own homes. My mother would not go outside after the curfew to fetch a piece of wood for our wood-heating stove for fear of being shot. I was too young to care, but my brothers and sister were barred from attending football games, basketball games, school dances, movies, and other social events, and they felt the restriction keenly. Min told me that he used to play poker with his friends, and if the game lasted beyond eight o'clock, he had to stay overnight wherever he was.

Hood River to Portland was a good two-hour drive back then.

Japanese Americans were thought not to be loyal enough to join the navy or marines, but a handful were able to enter the air force (which at that time was part of the army and did not become a separate branch of the military until after the war). Because Japanese American boys were being drafted and had to report to Portland, which was well over ten miles away, they'd be breaking the curfew. Each Japanese American inductee had to have a military escort to travel to Portland to the induction center. Hank Norimatsu was one of the Japanese American boys from Hood River who had to have one of these escorts.

The curfew met with resistance in the case of Min Yasui, a young man from Hood River. Everybody knew the Yasui family because the father had a general store downtown that sold a lot of Japanese goods like rice and soy sauce. Masuo Yasui had come to Seattle when he was 14 or so, when his brother was already living there. Mr. Yasui was one of the few first-generation Japanese people in Hood River who spoke English very well, with little or no accent. He and his wife were both well educated in Japan. The store in Hood River has become a historic place. It's still standing, and a lot has been written about it, but it's no longer a general store. I believe the block is now occupied by a restaurant.

The older Yasui kids were almost parallel in age to my siblings. The oldest son was about the age of Tot, the next son was about the age of my brother Min, all the way down to their youngest child, Yuka, who was a couple years older than I. I remember going into the Yasui store with my dad, and he and the owner would converse while I stared at the candy jar that was sitting on top of the glass showcase. When there'd be a pause in the conversation, Mr. Yasui would see my longing expression and offer me a free piece of candy. What a sweet memory.

When war broke out, his son Min Yasui had just graduated from the University of Oregon law school and was working for the Japanese consulate in Chicago. He protested the curfew as being a violation of his constitutional rights as a US citizen. Min Yasui roamed the streets of Portland and dared law enforcement officers to arrest him; he wanted to be a test case. They chose to ignore him at first, but he finally succeeded in being arrested. He was tried, convicted, and lodged in the Multnomah County jail, where he was kept for nine months in solitary confinement. He was not allowed to have a haircut, razor, fingernail clippers, or even a typewriter. He estimated that his case cost him and his family ten thousand dollars.

Years later, the cost swelled when he tried to get his conviction and sentence reversed or removed from the record. The process ended in 1987-88, when one last appeal was dropped after Min Yasui's death in 1987.[9] For his sacrifice in the name of principle, he was branded by some of the Japanese Americans of his generation as a draft dodger. When families were imprisoned in the government camps, Pa sought to gather donations for Min Yasui's legal defense fund and was met with derision and refusal from his peers.

It is no wonder that there are so few people in the world who have the courage of their convictions. They may live them out, only to be slapped in the face. Principle finds a very small following. For the most part, Japanese people were taught not to make waves but to "go with the flow." Actions like those of Min Yasui were more characteristic of individualistic American behavior. The more typically "well-behaved" Japanese found his defiance strange and uncomfortable.

In addition to the curfew, the sheriff's office gave us a list of contraband articles. By a certain date we were expected to collect any and all of the articles on the list that we owned and turn them in. They included cameras, shortwave radios, dynamite, firearms, swords, and more. We mostly delivered the contraband items to the sheriff's office as required.

After the specified date, the sheriff and his deputies came to our homes to see if we had "come clean." They searched our homes, barns, woodsheds, orchards, and every part of our houses to see that none of the contraband articles had been held back. If any such articles were discovered on the premises, the head of the household was seized and immediately taken away from his family and placed in an internment camp—a sort of detention center where these men were interrogated daily, I suppose by agents of the Federal Bureau of Investigation.

All orchardists had supplies of dynamite, which they used to blow up stumps of orchard trees that had become too old to bear fruit. Some farmers had forgotten about dynamite stored in barns or sheds, and they were arrested when it was found in their possession. My future sister-in-law Bessie's father, Mr. Watanabe, was one such person, taken away for having some dynamite in his barn. Some of these men were later reunited with their families in the "relocation centers" where all the rest of us were sent later. There were only five months between Pearl Harbor and our removal from Hood River, so I am sure most of the confiscations took place in January and February 1942. Because he was a prominent member of the Nikkei (Japanese emigrants and their descendants) community in Hood River, Masuo Yasui was taken away by FBI agents only five days after the Pearl Harbor attack.[10]

It became a common practice in many households for families to burn or otherwise destroy letters, diaries, photographs, books, magazines, family treasures (e.g., samurai swords), and other sentimental souvenirs or materials in the Japanese language—anything that linked them to Japan. Ma suggested burning a picture of her nephew, dressed in Japanese military uniform with a machine gun or some such weapon on the ground in front of him. We urged her not to do it—the only picture she had of her nephew. I still have that picture of my cousin in my possession. He died in the war, so I lost the opportunity of ever meeting him.

After our return to the West Coast in 1945 and World War II had ended, the confiscated contraband articles were returned to us. I saw once again the old Westinghouse shortwave radio and the Kodak camera with the accordion-pleated lens holder. The guns, explosives, and swords were not returned, but explained away as having been lost or unlocatable. Some of our neighbors recognized their own guns or rifles in the cabinets and collections of persons who were either friends of the sheriff or perhaps customers in a private auction. The firearms were old and outdated anyway, but the means of disposal did not meet with positive feelings from their former owners, to be sure.

In 1941, most of the Issei (first-generation Japanese born in Japan) were in their fifties and sixties, but because of their alien status, they did not enjoy full authority. Their children, even the oldest, were still teenagers or in their early twenties, but they were the ones who had to take over the leadership of their people. One 15-year-old San Franciscan's recollections of the outbreak of the war were echoed by my older brothers: It was just another incident in their lives, the curfew simply an inconvenience.

Executive Order 9066, issued by Franklin D. Roosevelt on February 19, 1942, authorized the removal of about 120,000 persons of Japanese ancestry from their homes on the West Coast and detainment in "assembly centers" and later in "relocation centers."[11] The exclusion zone consisted of the entire states of California and Alaska, nearly all of Oregon and Washington, and part of Arizona. This mass movement was referred to as "The Evacuation." Even the oldsters then and since have referred to that time in their lives by that label, an odd-sounding vocabulary item in their Japanese accent and limited English. In Pa's speech it sounded something like "Ebb-bock-EH-shone."

The executive order gave the War Department authority to define military areas in the western United States and to exclude from them "any or all persons" who would be "subject to whatever restrictions the Secretary of War or appropriate Military commander may impose in his discretion."[12] There was not one word about Japanese, Japanese Americans (most sources agree that roughly two-thirds of all those incarcerated were US citizens by birth, like me), or persons of Japanese ancestry. In fact, this was the only group of people who were moved out of their homes and confined under the government's jurisdiction. About 3,000 individuals of Italian ancestry and 11,500 with German background in the United States were placed in camps in Texas, North Dakota, and Hawaii,[13] but far fewer than all the Japanese immigrants and their children from the three Pacific coastal states.

One of the many ironies of the situation is that in Hawaii, where more than a third of the population consisted of Japanese immigrants and Japanese American citizens, and which was much closer to Japan and actually had been attacked by that nation, the local population was *not* rounded up like we were. There was a camp called Honouliuli, which held up to four thousand military prisoners of war,[14] and another at Kilauea Military Camp, but the several hundred Hawaiian prisoners of Japanese nationality or descent were religious leaders, business owners, citizens who had gone to Japan for their education, and other supposed threats among the community's leaders.[15] Otherwise, there were just too many Japanese and Japanese Americans in Hawaii to imprison them all; they were critical for the islands' economy.[16]

Which does not mean life was free and easy for them in Hawaii, either. The US Navy treated the islands as an "enemy country" (it was still a US territory then, not a state), where all the inhabitants were registered and underwent the first mass fingerprinting and vaccination campaign in US history. They were required to carry identification cards at all times, on pain of potential arrest, and University of Hawaii grads processed for their diplomas in cap, gown, and gas masks.[17]

I've occasionally been asked whether the evacuation was especially easy for the United States to do because the population was Japanese. I think so. I don't think the government knew that much about Japanese culture, though; it was just lucky, because the Japanese for the most part are pliable and compliant, and they do what they're told. Otherwise, the authorities might have had to deal with a substantial backlash.

Many Japanese Americans readily recognized the danger of the executive order for people from other racial and ethnic backgrounds. Through their organization, the Japanese American Citizens League, they labored and lobbied for many years after the war to have Executive Order 9066 rescinded. They felt that any other group in the future who might be labeled as someone "who might threaten the war effort" should be spared the experience of the Japanese Americans in World War II. A little over thirty years later, they finally accomplished their goal. In April 1976, President Gerald Ford signed the rescinding order.[18]

In 1942 and generally thereafter, the facilities were collectively known as "internment camps." Many books, websites, and Americans continue to refer to them by that phrase, but it is a misnomer. In international law, an "intern" is an alien enemy who has been captured and legally imprisoned under the terms of the Geneva Convention. The United States did intern enemy nationals in small camps located in Idaho, Montana, New Mexico, North Dakota, and Texas administered by the Department of Justice. The internees included more than 2,200 Japanese individuals that US authorities pressured Bolivia, Colombia, Costa Rica, Ecuador, Mexico, Nicaragua, Panama, and Peru to turn over because the government planned to use them as hostages to exchange for US prisoners of war held by Japan in the Pacific war.[19]

But two-thirds of us sent to the camps run by the War Relocation Authority under Executive Order 9066 in World War II were US citizens, and our parents were not exactly enemy aliens who had attacked this country and been captured. They had come of their free will to make their lives here. Densho Encyclopedia, an authoritative website devoted to preservation of the Japanese American legacy, and named after the Japanese word that means "to pass on to the next generation," recommends using the term "incarceration" instead of internment, and "concentration camp" for "internment camp."[20]

The latter substitution might offend some readers because "concentration camp" has become so closely associated with the Nazis and the facilities they administered for Jews, Roma, Jehovah's Witnesses, disabled individuals, homosexuals, and others, but those might more properly be called death camps or extermination camps. *Webster's New World Fourth College Edition* defines a concentration camp as "A camp in which political dissidents, members of minority ethnic groups, etc. are confined."[21] The *Oxford English Dictionary* also defines it as "A camp in which large numbers of people, esp. political prisoners or members of persecuted minorities, are deliberately imprisoned."[22] Even President Roosevelt referred to the camps he had ordered at the time as concentration camps.

I will avoid both the incorrect and the loaded terms and refer to each camp initially by its official title at the time (as well as some of the other euphemisms the authorities employed) in quotation marks. I also use the terms prison camp, incarceration camp, or just plain camp.

How was the United States going to house 120,000 people just like that? We would first be sent to "assembly centers," which were hurriedly prepared facilities capable of housing smaller numbers of people than the "relocation centers" that were being prepared for more permanent residence and to which we were later transferred. I call the first type "hurry up and lock 'em up" camps. There was only one in Washington, in Puyallup; and one in Oregon, at Vanport, an industrial area on the north side of Portland along the Columbia River.

Most of these assembly centers were former racetracks, fairgrounds, or abandoned army camps. Note that the first places were called "assembly centers," where they assembled us; then we were sent to "relocation centers" because we were being relocated. And instead of being referred to as persons, they called us "evacuees." These were sly euphemisms for a not-necessarily-legal operation.

We were told we could take only those family possessions that we could carry by ourselves. This amounted to about five hundred pounds for our family. My parents packed two big bags I could barely carry, because we didn't know how long we'd be gone. Each family was given a family number, and this number, written on tags, was attached to all our baggage and to each person in the family. Each of us in the Asai family was #16339, just like each piece of baggage.

Ma had rheumatism, for which I often gave her regular massages after a long day of work on the farm. (Sometimes I did this for Pa, too.) In the rush to pack for the evacuation, Ma fell down the stairs with a pillow in her arms. I saw her at the bottom of the stairway after the fall, clutching the pillow. After that injury, the rheumatism in her right arm caused her so much discomfort in camp that she had to sleep with her arm dangling over the side of the bed.

The government told us of a warehouse in Portland available for use by the Japanese people, to store any household goods we might wish to stow "for the duration," an expression that became familiar to us. It meant an undetermined time, an indefinite length of years, which kept us in a kind of suspension. The Japanese were not ready to trust the government at this point, even if the services were free, for they feared the eventual loss of their property, just as some of the contraband articles we had turned in to the sheriff's office would become "lost." Many preferred to take their chances and stored their belongings with friends or in a locked room of their homes, sheds, and barns.

We left our piano and living room rug with the Wallaces, a brother to our good neighbors, Carl and Hazel Smith. Mrs. Wallace was a teacher at Barrett School, my elementary school. We learned after the war that the warehouse storage had been a good idea and one we should have taken advantage of. Everything was handled carefully and taken care of, and returned to the owners after the war. How were we to know we could count on the government in this matter—the same government that was pulling us from our homes and confining us in camps?

I don't know anything about the families who leased our main orchard and lived in our house. The

Carl and Hazel Smith, staunch allies of Japanese Americans in Hood River, during and after the war (Asai family collection)

person who leased the orchard had the right to do whatever he wanted with the house or the land, but our friend Carl Smith kind of oversaw what was happening there. Carl would see to it that the residents were called out on any untoward actions. The idea I got was that the person who leased the property was to give my father a certain percentage of the profits: maybe 80-20 or something like that. I presume the money went to the bank. But somehow, for three years, no net profit was reported, which we knew was a lie. So for the years we were in camp, we had no income.

We were told to pack and be ready, but not until we got on the train to be sent to who-knew-where did my 24-year-old brother Min finally accept that it was going to happen. The approximately three-hundred-plus Japanese Americans from Hood River were taken to Pinedale Assembly Center near Fresno. When we left Hood River on May 13, 1942, several friends came to bid us good-bye while we were still in our homes. Many came to the train depot in town when our train pulled out. I remember wondering if any of my classmates were going to come to say goodbye to me at the train station and hoping they would, but nobody came, probably because it was during the school day and they had to be in class. I remember how empty I felt, but in later years I thought, well, that wasn't their fault. Maybe they wanted to come and say goodbye but they didn't know.

Ralph Sherrieb, the owner-proprietor of a general store near our home, West Side Store, came to our house, shed tears as he said goodbye, and gave us an address book as a farewell gift, entreating us to write letters to him. But three years later, when we returned home from camp, his store had a "No Jap Trade" sign hanging on the door.

At first, I felt excited about "going to camp," imagining it to be some kind of extended vacation trip. This would be my first train ride. When we boarded the train, we were instructed to pull the blinds and not to peek out of the windows. This ruined the pleasure of my first train ride considerably, and it certainly caused all the parents a great deal of trouble. The journey from Hood River, Oregon, to Fresno, California, is a long train trip, and trying to keep the curious eyes of children from wandering in forbidden directions was not easy. All that time we were traveling and not knowing where we were going, with the blinds closed.

There were soldiers on the train with us, ostensibly to keep us in line. Along the way, our train was sidetracked several times as we made way for troop trains that took priority on the rails. We did not know where we were being taken, how long we'd be on the train, how long we could expect to be away from our homes in Oregon; the uncertainties were many. Our parents were flooded with normal children's questions:

Where are we now?
Where are we going?
How much longer do we have to be on the train?
When will we go home?
Why do we have to be here?
Why can't we look out the window?

and on and on. To these questions there were no answers except: "I don't know."

Min Yasui's sister Michi was a senior at the University of Oregon in Eugene when the war came. Their brother Shu was also there for his freshman year. When they heard about the possibility that our families would be removed from our homes and put in camps, Michi figured the train would come through Eugene. So she ran down to the railroad tracks and waited in hopes of seeing her mother, brother, and sister. (Her father, Mr. Yasui, was already in a special prison camp at Fort Sill, Oklahoma, where four hundred Japanese men were housed in tents.)[23] But since we had been instructed to keep the blinds closed, if the train went through Eugene and the Yasuis were on it, Michi probably couldn't see them.

Later that year, Michi was supposed to graduate from the university, but the commencement ceremonies were held at night due to the war. Because of the curfew at the time, she couldn't attend her own graduation. She eventually became a teacher in the Denver area. Decades later, her unawarded diploma turned up in the University of Oregon archives. Invited by the university to receive it in an upcoming commencement, Michi Yasui Ando said thanks but no thanks. She eventually agreed to return to Oregon and receive her diploma in 1986. I attended that event, which would be the last time I saw Min Yasui, who died later that year.

Many from the Los Angeles area were housed at the Santa Anita Racetrack, where the previous inhabitants had left behind their distinctive odors. Someone told us that the Japanese who lived there displayed their humor by having a sign contest, with such entrants as "Dung Palace," "Manure Mansion," and others of similarly graphic connotation. The signs were tacked up over the doorway of their one-, two- or three-horse-stall apartments. My future sister-in-law Bessie Watanabe said her first thought upon arriving at the assembly center was, "This is your home."

There were seven in our family at Pinedale Assembly Center: Pa, Ma, Min, Mika, Gene, Dick, and me. If you already had two sons in the army (and we did—Tot and Half), it was treated as a hardship for the family to draft any more. So Min had been reclassified from 1-A to 4-C (aliens not subject to military service) and went with us to Pinedale. His 4-C classification was not changed back to 1-A until 1945. The army later encouraged and accepted volunteers out of the camps, but no one was drafted out of the Pinedale camp at this time.

Our family lived in one large room with seven army cots and mattresses. One or two khaki blankets were allotted to each bed. We used our own sheets. We felt lucky in later camps when we heard that in some places, the Japanese were given mattress ticking and had to fill it themselves with straw.

We were housed in barracks with tarpaper nailed onto the exterior walls with lathlike sticks. The rooms were partitioned but open above the rafters, so we could hear the neighbors' conversations, domestic quarrels, and lovers' tête-à-têtes. This situation fed the Japanese thirst for gossip perfectly. If we wanted to be especially mischievous, we could contrive a way to climb or be lifted up high enough to peek over the rafters and into the lives of our neighbors.

Every night for a few weeks, there was a curfew and head count. For two or three months we received a clothing allowance, and a book of scrip or coupons worth about $6.00 for adults, $3.75 for older children, and $1.75 for young ones. These coupons could be spent in the camp canteen for candy, gum, socks, writing supplies, toothpaste, or whatever few items were available in the camp store.

Most people around us were from the temperate climates of the Pacific Northwest like us, unaccustomed to the heat of Fresno. Some days in the hundred-degree-plus weather we could do nothing but sit and fan ourselves. Some persons fainted in the hot sun while waiting in line to eat in the mess hall. Some nights were so hot that we threw water on the concrete floor and slept on it, after pulling our mattresses off our beds. Our clothes faded from the hot sun, which was another thing we were not used to.

In order to receive the coupon books, Pa had to stand in line in that hundred-degree weather. When they were discontinued, he was not unhappy about it. We children had a hard time sleeping at night in such heat and complained about being put to bed at the usual hour, heat or no heat. A few times the camp authorities gave each family a block of ice. We set the block in the middle of the concrete floor and sat around it to cool off, chipping off pieces to suck.

The security precautions at the assembly center were extensive. A fine-meshed fence rose from the ground to about eight or ten feet, and above that were three or four rows of electrified barbed wire. The fences were right up close to the barracks, so when you looked out the window you were having to stare at this eight-foot-high fence.

At each corner of the camp were watch towers manned twenty-four hours a day by sentries (US military police, many of them less than enthusiastic about their duty, if not sheepish). From these towers shone searchlights after dark, which moved over the tar-papered barracks all night. As I lay in bed, I could feel the searchlight cross my face in spite of my closed eyes as it made its wide, measured, predictable sweep over the camp: one-two-three-four-five-SIX, one-two-three-four-five-SIX. After we moved to the "relocation center" at Tule Lake, where there was no searchlight, I still saw the light through closed eyes, even in my sleep. It was a few months' time before I could rid myself of the searchlight's image—one-two-three-four-five-SIX—that was imprinted on my brain.

My mother would say, "Now don't go anywhere near the fence," because we figured if we got close to the fence, they were going to shoot us. As I look back, I realize that we small children wanted to believe that the sentry in the searchlight tower was a human being and not a soldier with a gun who would shoot us if we made any suspicious moves. The first time we lost the ball over the fence, since I was the talkative one, I was elected to ask the MP in the tower to retrieve our ball. So I went over to the tower and shouted up to him, "We lost our ball across the fence. Could you get it for us?" And he smiled. He came down the stairs off the tower and walked down the road to get the ball and threw it over the fence to us.

I can still remember that first experience and thinking, *Those guys aren't mean guys. They're not going to shoot us. They're just human beings with a job to do, and he just happens to be stuck up there, trying to guard us.* We would make a kind of game of it—sometimes we'd throw the ball over the fence on purpose. If he was good-looking, the girls would see to it that the ball got over the fence more often than accident could explain. The sentry probably realized this and took it all in good humor, perhaps flattered to think that the girls wanted to see him up close again.

Across the road from the camp was a fig orchard. I had never seen a fresh fig growing, never touched or eaten one, and I was curious about those figs. Once a sentry picked a fig and handed it to me, but it was too early to be harvested, so the fig was inedible. It did satisfy my curiosity, if not my hunger, for figs.

Pinedale suffered from a shortage of toilets, shower heads, and sinks in the public restrooms and shower houses. People had to line up to wait their turn. The lavatories had six or eight toilet seats side by side, with another row of six or eight back-to-back on the other side. There were no partitions in the lavatories and showers. Those who were modest had to make painful adjustments for the lack of privacy.

Most Japanese families had minimum inhibition regarding nudity, perhaps because most of the Japanese who came to America were from a rural background. In any case, children who had had no experience seeing other people outside their own family in the nude, or being seen themselves, were readily exposed to both situations.

In the restroom, a large wall poster faced the toilet seat. On it were large drawings of a male and female scorpion. The poster was intended to help you distinguish the dangerous female scorpion from the harmless male. We were instructed to lift the seat and examine the toilet before sitting down. That, plus the drawing on the wall, discouraged people from lingering in the lavatories. This was no place for the bathroom reader.

My future sister-in-law Bessie Watanabe recalled that the ladies' and men's restrooms rotated in shifts on some occasions, and no one could remember who was supposed to be using the facilities when. There was a lot of confusion. At night, sleep was disturbed by the sound of drilling and ditch digging, when the workers hit the hardpan in the soil while constructing more lavatories to accommodate the growing number of prisoners.

Chlorine foot baths were provided for us to step in before going into the communal shower. How they did sting the feet, especially if you had a cut or a sore! Children had to be monitored, for they hated to use the chlorine bath. In spite of these precautions, athlete's foot was a problem for many.

We had been used to soft water in Oregon. The water in Pinedale was so hard that it was not easy to get clothes or hair clean. We used more soap and shampoo than we were used to, hoping for suds and lather, but to no avail. Worst of all, it was difficult to get the soap rinsed out of both hair and clothes. Shampoo was not always available either, which meant that we used toilet soap to wash our hair sometimes.

On rare occasions, the camp store would get a stock of yard

goods in. The news spread like wildfire, and everyone rushed to the store to buy whatever had come in. A few days or weeks later, one could see many people sporting new shirts, blouses, or dresses all in the same pattern, made from the yardage.

Min began working in the camp commissary, loading and unloading food boxes for the camp. He also was given a short lesson on how to make pies in the camp bakery. The bakery made mostly fruit pies for consumption by the camp inhabitants. The heat of the ovens added to the scorching temperatures outside. Bessie, who became his wife years later, remembered that young men who worked in the commissary had fringe benefits, such as being able to bring home grapefruit. They would shout, "Here comes a grapefruit!" and with no further warning, a grapefruit would come flying over the rafters into the neighbors' room.

As soon as the call for laborers came from sugar beet farmers in Utah, Min applied and was among the first Nisei to leave the assembly center, in July 1942. He worked in and around Ogden in the sugar beet fields, as well as in a chemistry lab. The lab job made use of the chemistry education he had received at Linfield College and Oregon State College. From working in the lab, Min's desire to continue his studies grew. He moved to Chicago in hopes of both finding a job and being able to return to school. He did find a job and went to night school at the University of Chicago for a couple of terms to study chemistry further.

Mrs. Hirasawa, a friend from Hood River, left Pinedale in a pine box. She was so opposed to the idea of being taken from her home in Hood River that she had to be forcibly removed by her family to board the train that took us to that first camp. She became a little hysterical there and was never the same again. She died in Pinedale not long after her arrival.

We stayed in the "assembly center" at Pinedale about four months. In September 1942, the "relocation center" was ready for us. The Japanese families of Hood River were separated then; some went to Minidoka near Twin Falls, Idaho, some to Topaz in Utah, and some to Jerome and Rohwer in Arkansas. Our family was sent to Tule Lake, in Northern California, just south of the border from Klamath Falls, Oregon.

CHAPTER 8

Tule Lake "Relocation Camp"

The first permanent camp to open was Manzanar in Owens Valley, California, in March 1942. Construction began on Tule Lake in mid-April, and that camp officially opened on May 27, which shows you how fast the process was. Tule Lake initially housed Issei, Nisei, and Sansei (third-generation Japanese Americans) from Sacramento County, California (a total of 4,984), King County, Washington (2,703), and 425 from our Hood River County contingent.[1]

I do not remember the trip we made from Fresno to Tule Lake in July 1942. We reached Tule Lake and were given two rooms that were smaller than the one in Pinedale for our family of six, Min now being gone to the sugar beet farms in Utah. By September, the camp had a population of about 15,000, but it would peak with nearly 19,000 residents thereafter—almost 4,000 more than the camp was built to handle.[2] Over the four years it would be open, Tule Lake would hold 29,840 people.[3] The removal of all 120,000 persons from their homes in the Western military exclusion zone to ten inland camps was completed by August 18, 1942.[4]

Tule Lake had seventy-four residential blocks divided into eight wards. Each block contained fourteen barracks that measured 20 × 100 × 120 feet, and every barrack housed five to seven families,[5] for

Tule Lake, past (archival camp photo) and present (when I visited in 2014)
(Loftus family collection)

an average of three hundred people in each block. The buildings
were still tar-papered structures. Each barrack contained five or six
rooms, and three entries. A room had a single light bulb hanging
from the ceiling, a coal-burning pot-bellied stove, and up to eight
cots for sleeping. A door connected the rooms to form a kind of
suite. You might enter one door and there'd be one family on one
side and another family on the other. There were no wallboards or
ceilings, just the construction, so you could see rafters everywhere.
There was no plumbing of any kind, only the heating stove for
the winter. We didn't have any place to put things, but since the
two-by-fours along the doors and the windows were exposed, we
used those for shelves. I remember putting all my little things on
the two-by-fours.

By this time, the authorities had realized we were not going to be
difficult to keep locked up, so the fences were placed far away from
the camp. If you strained your eyes, you could perhaps make out

three rows of barbed wire like the kind you'd have to keep a cow in a pasture. So if you were a high jumper, you could jump over. Or if you were small like me, you could lie on your stomach and just ease out through the lower barbed wire. But they were electrified, so you didn't want to touch it. You didn't have to look at it like in Pinedale, though, so it wasn't so bad. You could not leave the camp unless you went through the official entrance, where MPs were guarding the gate. There was a guy with a gun there, to make sure the right people were going in and out. They needed to know where you were going and what you were going for.

Camp authorities allowed residents who were American citizens to leave and go shopping in Klamath Falls. You could get on a bus and go to town. My sister did it once and said it was so unfriendly in Klamath Falls that she never went again. I don't think I ever went through that gate, from the time I went in to live in the camp until I left permanently.

In the middle of each block was a community lavatory with laundry room, ironing room, and showers. At one end of the block was a mess hall. The block office was where mail was delivered and where most of the activity, social and otherwise, centered. Our mail was put into boxes there, and we checked them every day to see if we had received any mail. Not having any plumbing in our rooms, night visits to the toilets were sometimes postponed to avoid getting out of a warm bed and walking in the cold night air. I would guess that there were many "accidents" for families with small children who had to go to the bathroom at night.

Some blocks also had a recreation hall where ping pong, chess, and bull sessions could be engaged in. In our block in Tule Lake, some clever person found a wagon wheel out in the field, erected a pole, and mounted the wheel on top. Then he hung ropes down from it to make a deluxe Maypole. There were huge knots in the ropes to grasp it securely, but my hands were too small to go around the thick rope. On my first try at the Maypole, I was flying out from the pole at about thirty degrees, lost my hold, and fell flat on my stomach, which knocked the wind out of me.

We ate in the mess halls, where whole blocks of residents ate together. You could go to somebody else's block and eat there, where you didn't live, but the administration discouraged the practice because food was allocated for the number of people in each block. We lined up cafeteria-style to get our plates of food in the mess hall. Plates of relish or carrot sticks or bread would be placed on the tables for us. Each table seated about twelve to fifteen persons. It was first come, first served, and if you were the last to be seated, you might have to go without bread or carrot sticks. One learned to rush to empty tables rather than search for tables where friends were already sitting—the choice depending on which hunger you were suffering from the most, physical or social. A large sign hung over the dining hall admonishing us to "eat slowly for the sake of your health." This sign was the object of jokes and laughter. If you lingered too long at the table, you would find yourself with several people waiting around you to clear the table and get you out of there so that they could go home from their KP duty.

The food served in the mess hall was adequate. There was plenty of it, but like all institutional food, it was often criticized. The complaints I recall most often had to do with foods that were not part of the typical Japanese diet. Rutabagas cooked and mashed looked like mashed yams. Japanese love yams, but the look of negative surprise when they spooned their first bit of rutabagas, expecting the taste of yams, still sticks in my mind. Turnips met with the same lack of enthusiasm, especially from the younger Japanese.

Jams and jellies were seldom served, but we always had orange marmalade. Although I will eat orange marmalade today in small quantities, the memory of three years of orange marmalade in place of raspberry or strawberry jam and grape jelly has had a permanent effect. Apple butter was also provided and was just about as popular as orange marmalade. Most persons preferred only butter.

The worst part was that the Japanese family unit began to break down. The old folks expected the kids to sit with them every night at dinner. Who wants to sit and eat dinner with Mom and Dad when you can be with all your friends? So parents had a hard time; some tried to force their children to stay with them, but they couldn't do it. My father was a progressive, liberal-minded, and freedom-loving man, so he didn't force us to do things the way many other Issei did with their children. But I was a little girl, so I tended to sit with my parents in Pinedale and Tule Lake, until I was in the third camp at Heart Mountain. You get into your teen years and begin to assume you're an adult who can do whatever she wants, and I think I probably wandered away from my family then. But my parents didn't say or do anything to prevent that.

The camp also had a movie theater, which was just another barrack with bleachers or risers for seats. When you sat away up in the back, your head hit the ceiling if you stood up. On hot days the heat back there was unbearable, but dating couples were willing to suffer the heat for the small amount of privacy the back rows afforded. The noisy, teasing children were far in front of them.

Church services, both Buddhist and Christian, were available in barracks. I remember going to the Christian Sunday school, but I don't remember my dad going to the Buddhist events.

"Grow a victory garden; help win the war," we were told. Pa worked as a foreman on one of the largest victory gardens in the country, which raised vegetables for camp use. He boarded a truck to leave camp through the gate and supervised crews in fields outside the camp on acreage to the north and west. The men would work all day, then come back on the truck. We raised all the vegetables we needed to feed our camps, and the surplus was shipped all over the country to feed other hungry Americans, as part of the Japanese Americans' share in the war effort.

Tule Lake had once been two lakes, but the US Bureau of Reclamation had drained one of them in 1920 to create farming homesteads. The lake bottom was primarily where Tule Lake camp was built. By digging in the sand, one could sift out thousands of shells. The women soaked these shells in a bucket of Clorox bleach until they were white and used them to make shell pictures, pins, corsages, and other decorative articles with the various shapes of shells, painting them with colored fingernail polish or just clear lacquer to make them shiny. For many of these women, this was the first time they had done a craft like this. Having been farmers' wives for the most part, they had never had time for such leisure activities. My mother made jewelry in 1942-43 out of shells dug out of the lake bottom.

The other, existing lake attracted a tremendous number of wild geese and ducks. My dad said there were so many birds, you could just reach down and pick them up. So he did. Everyone who worked was issued coats and jackets—military surplus clothes—but I believe Pa wore an old Levi jacket with huge pockets that was sent to him by one of my brothers in the army. Farmers were even issued army work shoes. Garbage collectors received rubber pants, gloves, and shirts. Pa brought home one or two birds, wrapped in wax paper from his sack lunch, carefully hiding it in the pockets of his work jacket. We had a bird dinner that nobody else got to enjoy.

During these Tule Lake victory garden days, Pa also brought home a kind of mushroom or fungi, which we cooked in our room. We went to the mess hall and got our ration of rice to go with the mushrooms and cooked on the coal-heating stove provided for our rooms. On occasion we used a hot plate, which one of my brothers sent to us at some time during our stay in camp. The illegal birds and wild mushrooms were extra tasty as a change from the institutional food we ate every day.

Ma worked in the mess doing KP work: peeling potatoes, washing dishes, and clearing tables. Any professional people such as doctors and dentists were required to work in the camp clinic and/ or hospital. Everyone received a standard wage of sixteen dollars a month, no matter what job. No pay was to exceed that for US soldiers (i.e., twenty-one dollars a month). The only professionally trained persons not allowed to do their work were teachers. They were allowed to be teachers' aides to Caucasian teachers who were brought into the camp from "outside."

At one time Ma worked as a domestic in the camp housing area for administrators. She walked to the edge of the camp to clean the apartments of the Caucasian administrators' families' homes. She had never seen a clothes hamper before and did not know what it was. In our home, a cardboard box was what we used for dirty clothes. When I returned to Tule Lake in 2006 for a reunion of people who had been kept there, I met the son of the camp's superintendent of schools, a Caucasian boy who had been in the fifth grade with me. We were both 74 years old now, and he had come all the way from Madison, Wisconsin, where he had retired as head of the department of medicine at the university there. He had married a Japanese American woman and received a grant to do two years of medical research in Hiroshima.

During our days in camp, Pa went to the post office for our postal needs. He told me he had a hard time obtaining postcards, which he referred to as "postal paper" to the clerk, who had to guess Pa's meaning. To write to our brothers in the army overseas, we used "V-Mail," a single-sheet, fold-up letter and envelope in one, similar to present-day aerograms.

Most Japanese people have trouble sounding out the letter V. It requires one to press the upper teeth against the lower lips, and in Japan you don't even want your mouth to be seen in the first place! One day I saw and heard Pa reading the newspaper and with great effort contorting his mouth to make strange sounds, something like "boo-eeee, boo-eeee." I asked him what he was doing. He explained that the newspaper gave a formula for pronouncing the letter V correctly, and he was trying it out.

I told him no, it's not "boo-eeee," it's "vee." Even seeing me do that, he couldn't do it, because he was unaccustomed to putting his teeth out in the open. If only I had had the training I would receive in the mid-1950s for teaching English as a Second Language, I could have done a better job with Pa than the newspaper did in the early 1940s. Since then, I have helped many Asian students to pronounce that sound, one which poses a challenge for Japanese, Chinese, Korean, and even Spanish natives.

Since Ma wrote no English and Pa wrote little and with difficulty, it was the children's duty to keep up a correspondence with our brothers in the army and all our friends back in Hood River. Ma told me what to say to Tot and Half, and I regularly wrote letters to them. I was in the fourth and fifth grade then. Umbrellas were scarce because of the metal skeletons in them (all metal was reserved for the war effort), and I remember Ma's repeated reminders to ask my brothers to send us an umbrella. This was to protect us from the oppressive heat of California and later the snow and rain in Wyoming.

During our stay in Tule Lake, my eldest brother received a month's furlough before going overseas. Tule Lake camp was within the "wartime restricted zone" and therefore off limits to Tot, so he could not come to us. Instead, he visited some hometown friends at the Minidoka Relocation Center near Twin Falls, Idaho, which was outside the restricted zone to the east. It was November 1942, and he said he sank down into the mud between the barracks where the Japanese lived. The roads around the camp were also muddy.

Half and Tot received twenty-one dollars a month in the army. Ten dollars of Half's paycheck came to us in the form of a "dependency check." My parents turned these checks over to Mika each month, to enable her to go to Latter-Day Saints Business College (which was renamed Ensign College in 2020) in Salt Lake City. She worked for her room and board with the Jones family, doing some housework and caring for their three young sons. Mr.

Jones was in the navy. In addition to her room and board, Mika received three dollars a week. She remembered how nicely Mrs. Jones treated her and the closeness she felt toward the family. Mika named her first child after the Jones's youngest son, Steve.

A little later, thirty-seven dollars was deducted from Tot's army paycheck to be sent home to us as a dependency check. I believe this too was sent on to Mika. She completed the business course in nine months and worked as a secretary in Salt Lake City and later Portland, where she was living when the rest of the family was allowed to go back to our native Oregon in the spring of 1945.

That first Christmas in camp (1942) was memorable in that we might have been the only ones in the whole Tule Lake camp who had a bona fide fir Christmas tree. In California, the trees were not shaped like Christmas trees ought to be (at least in 1942 this was so). All the trees available were tall, linear, and looked more like an inverted ice cream cone than a pyramid or triangle with a wide skirt.

Our good friends the Roy Hays drove to Tule Lake from Hood River with a fir tree cut from our own wooded property, to serve as our Christmas tree. I don't think I will ever forget how we felt when they brought us that tree. I don't remember what we had to decorate it, but that didn't seem important then.

In early February 1943, all aliens and citizens of age in the camps were made to answer a questionnaire. In it were two questions deemed most crucial in terms of what were considered matters of loyalty. Question 27 asked:

Are you willing to serve in the armed forces of the United States on combat duty, wherever ordered?

Question 28:
Will you swear unqualified allegiance to the United States of America and faithfully defend the United States from any and all attack by foreign or domestic forces, and forswear any

form of allegiance to the Japanese Emperor or any other foreign government, power, or organization?

Every man and boy, 17 years old and up, had to answer, including my father, who was by this time 69 years old. In response to question 27, many said, "The hell I will; you know where you can put *that*." Others said, "I'll go! Anything to get out of this hellhole!"

Question 28 asked if the person would *forswear* allegiance to a foreign nation and pledge complete allegiance to the United States. Most Nisei had never had any allegiance to Japan to begin with, so if they answered "yes" to that question, that would seem to indicate that they once had. "No" would certainly not be an answer that fit their feelings, so neither answer seemed appropriate. I don't know a single second-generation Japanese American who had *any* allegiance to the Japanese emperor. Many of them couldn't even speak Japanese, and they were incensed to be asked such a question. For us, it was kind of like asking, "When did you stop beating your wife?" Some of the Nisei boys let their anger get the best of them and answered no to both questions.

The aliens like my parents, although they were Japanese citizens, had come to the United States to live their lives as Americans but were denied citizenship despite having lived here for decades. At that point, Ma and Pa had been settled here for thirty-three and forty years, respectively. Furthermore, the sons of many of these couples had volunteered for or been drafted into the US Army, which was the case with our family, while their parents were locked up in camps. A few men of that older generation had volunteered to serve in World War I with the hope of becoming US citizens, but the successful ones had a long legal fight afterward, and many failed.[6] (At least nine Issei had even served in the Spanish-American War back in 1896, so it's conceivable that vets from that conflict ended up in the camps, too.[7])

Understandably, many felt indignant about being asked to declare complete faith and loyalty to the government of a nation that had done these things to them. The Japanese and Japanese Americans had been conditioned to distrust anything the US government said. It was not unlike the broken treaties between European immigrants and the Native Americans.

Nearly 75,000 people filled out the questionnaire, and about 6,700 answered no to questions 27 and 28. The answers to these two questions were the determining factor as to whether an individual was kept at Tule Lake, which would be turned into a "segregation center," or transferred to one of several other "relocation centers." Persons were labeled "no-no's," "yes-yeses," "no-yeses," and "yes-no's" based on their answers to these two questions. The "no-no's" were deemed "disloyal," and the "yes-yeses" were classified as "loyal."

Some people answered yes-no or no-yes, which puzzled the army. Those with mixed answers were called in for interviews, where they were questioned and then sorted into the "loyal" or "disloyal" groups on the basis of the interview. The peculiar thing was that each person was given a certain amount of time after filling out the questionnaire the first time to think it over and go back and change the answers if desired.

My father was a Zen Buddhist. He never let his emotions get away with him. Pa's suspicions as to the intent of these questionnaires were very close to what eventually happened. He answered yes-yes right away, which meant we would be transferred from Tule Lake to Heart Mountain, Wyoming. All the no-no's from the other nine "relocation centers" were sent to Tule Lake. The camp almost doubled in population after the loyalty questionnaire and the no-no's from the other nine camps were moved in.

When people hear "Tule Lake," they say, "Oh, I heard about that place, where the awful things happened." When I was there, none of that was the case, because the loyalty oath hadn't been administered yet. After we were shifted to Wyoming, the army changed Tule Lake camp to a segregation center. You can imagine an entire camp full of angry and indignant no-no's.

My Caucasian classmate, the son of the school superintendent, told me in 2006 that he had been prohibited from going to school in the camp with the Japanese kids because they were regarded as dangerous. The army brought in a battalion of a thousand military police with armored cars and tanks.[8] A lighted seven-foot chain-link fence topped with barbed wire was erected, and the number of guard towers increased from six to twenty-eight.[9]

Camp officials built a stockade for one hundred men, in which two to three hundred of the most belligerent inmates were housed, with no plumbing and no windows. When I visited the structure in 2006, I was shocked to see dried blood stains on the stockade wall, and to read reports that they found baseball bats with blood on them. It seemed just like Guantanamo Bay, but in 1943 and 1944. This period was the basis for Ed Miyakawa's novel *Tule Lake*, after it had become a bad place.[10]

Riots occurred, and in November 1943, a month after my family had been moved to Heart Mountain in Wyoming, martial law was declared at Tule Lake. That remained in place only until mid-January of 1944, but shortly after martial law was removed, to add insult to injury, the army began to issue draft notices to the prisoners at Tule Lake. When twenty-seven men ignored the notice to report for their physicals, they were put on trial for violating the Selective Service Act. Even US District Court Judge Louis Goodman, who dismissed the case, *US vs. Masaaki Kuwabara*, was appalled. "It is shocking to the conscience that an American citizen be confined on the ground of disloyalty and then, while so under duress and restraint, be compelled to serve in the armed forces, or be prosecuted for not yielding to such compulsion," he wrote.[11]

Back in the spring of 1943, Pa visited many homes of those known to be no-no's. He tried to talk reason with them, encouraging them to answer yes-yes for their own good, but most of them were too filled with rage and indignation. He said to Mr. Sato, "Are you sure you want to answer 'no-no'? You might find yourself behind the gates of Yokohama when the war's over."

And he wasn't too far from wrong. Some persons who stuck by their no-no answers were sent to Japan after World War II. Minor children—American citizens by birth—became the unwilling victims of their parents' decision to answer no-no. They had been born here, grew up here, and didn't know anything about Japanese culture or the language, but had to go to Japan because they were minors and their parents had been judged "disloyal." (This is not dissimilar to the experience of the Dreamers, children of undocumented immigrants from Central and South America today.) A civil rights attorney in the United States, Wayne M. Collins, worked for twenty-three years to overturn more than four thousand cases in which US citizenship had been renounced, and saved more than a thousand individuals from being deported.[12]

I know of one young man who lost his citizenship because he was taken to Japan from Hood River before the war. I believe his mother, Mrs. Hachiya, was a picture bride who had come from Japan like Ma. Her maiden name was Komano Yasuhara. The Hachiya family was close friends with ours. Mrs. Hachiya wanted a girl in the worst way, and she had two sons, Frank and Homer. She kind of adopted me as her little girl, making dresses for me. In fact, I think I still have one dress that she made for me when I was small that today I keep on my big doll.

Mrs. Hachiya was so homesick—she kept saying, "I wanna go home, I wanna go home." My father counseled her and said, "Your place is here with your husband," and he advised her against returning to Japan. But she couldn't stand it, so she left with her younger son Homer, who wanted to stay with his dad, but went back to Japan before the war. Mr. Hachiya was very sad about it, but he was not a typical Japanese man who would insist, "You can't do that." She cried and was so lonely that he relented. I was still preschool age, so it was before 1941, but I don't remember how many years before that.

Homer grew up bilingual—he was my brother Gene's classmate in seventh or eighth grade—but because he went to Japan with his mother, he lost his US citizenship. He came back to Hood River as an adult and visited us, telling us he had worked for the Army of Occupation as a linguist after the war. Homer Hachiya had had to spend something like ten thousand dollars through the courts to get his citizenship back so he could return to the United States. When I went to Japan on a Fulbright scholarship, Homer was one of the people I visited, because by that time he had returned to Japan and married. He lived in Yokohama. He had two or three daughters and bought a home in Anaheim, California, so they could live in it and go to college here. I believe Homer finally returned to the United States and died in California.

Meanwhile, his older brother Frank, after studying in Japan for four years, returned to the University of Oregon to major in political science. Frank enlisted after Pearl Harbor and had served in the Pacific for three years when, on nearly the last day of 1944, he was in Leyte with the 32nd Infantry Regiment and volunteered to interrogate a newly captured Japanese prisoner of war. Crossing a valley to contact the forward unit with the prisoner, Frank Hachiya was shot under confusing circumstances—either enemy or "friendly" fire—through the liver, but he staggered up the hill to deliver the information he had gathered about enemy positions and troops to his commanding officer. He died four days later, on January 3, 1945, and was posthumously awarded the Silver Star with bronze cluster for gallantry in action and the Distinguished Service Cross.

Initially buried in the Armed Forces Cemetery on Leyte, Frank Hachiya's remains were returned to Hood River more than three years later, through the efforts of his father, a Red Cross supervisor who befriended him on Eniwetok named Monroe Sweetland, and Ray Yasui of the Hood River chapter of the Japanese American Citizens League. On September 11, 1948, Frank was laid to rest in Idlewilde Cemetery in Hood River next to my brother Half, who was a classmate of his. *The Oregonian* reported about two hundred friends and relations from the Japanese American community were in attendance at the memorial service, as well as a hundred others, including military dignitaries. Sweetland, by that time editor of the *Newport News*, and Martha Ferguson McKeown, a lifelong friend of Frank's who had become state regent of the Daughters of the American Revolution, both spoke at the service, as did my brother Min.[13]

"Love of country was foremost in his mind," Min said. "Little we realized as we wrestled and played together that he would prove it with his life. . . . We as citizens will fight to maintain the ideals and principles for which he died." My family took flowers to Frank's grave every time we visited the Asai family graves, for which his parents were grateful.

The confusion and controversy in the Japanese American community over the loyalty questions in the Tule Lake questionnaire created a huge division between the men that took decades to heal. The ones who said yes-yes and went into military service regarded the no-no's who didn't serve as disloyal. And the ones who said no to the questions felt it took a lot more courage to fight the US government on constitutional grounds than to just enter the army and go where it ordered you. The Japanese American community is still trying to heal those hard feelings.

CHAPTER 9

Heart Mountain "Relocation Camp"

Since Pa had answered yes-yes, we were moved from Tule Lake to Heart Mountain. Min had gotten out to work the Utah sugar beet farms and moved on to Chicago, so our family was down to six. A page titled "Final Reconciliation of All Train Lists" at Tule Lake Center says family #16339, camp address 6715-CD, consists of Sagoro, Matsu, Mika, Gene, Itsuo (Dick), and Mitsuko Asai. We were scheduled for Train 34, destination "Ht. Mt."[1]

We went north to Oregon, then east to Wyoming. That train trip I do remember, for it took us along the Washington side of the Columbia River. What made it such an emotional trip was that the train stopped just across the Columbia from Hood River, and boxes of Hood River apples were brought out and distributed to us on the train. We were looking across the river, pointing out the high school, our farm, and other familiar landmarks in our hometown to our friends in the train. We were so overcome with tears that we could not eat our apples.

The Heart Mountain Relocation Center was located in northwestern Wyoming between the small towns of Cody and Powell. The site was an isolated 730 acres surrounded by barbed wire on 46,000 acres owned by the Bureau of Reclamation. The camp ballooned the state's total number of Japanese immigrants and descendants as well as the state's population altogether. Before the war, only 643 Japanese people lived in Wyoming; at its height on January 1, 1943, (ten months before my family arrived), Heart Mountain camp housed 10,767 inmates[2] and qualified as the state's third-largest city.[3]

Built between the start of June and August 1942, Heart Mountain comprised 650 buildings and 467 residential barracks—all supplied with electricity, which was unusual for structures anywhere in the state at the time. But because the army gave the camp's chief engineer only sixty days to create the facility, many of the buildings were poorly constructed, with cracks between wallboards that were terrible protection against severe winters, when temperatures might dip to negative 30 degrees. Workers bragged they could erect an apartment barrack in fifty-eight minutes.[4]

Heart Mountain accepted its first residents on August 12, 1942.[5] A US Department of the Interior ledger titled "Name by Name Accounting of All Residents," dated December 1944, states that the Asai family arrived on October 3, 1943.[6]

For this move we received shots against Rocky Mountain tick fever. Any hikes in this camp had to be followed by a hot bath and careful examination of the body to get rid of the ticks, which lodged themselves all over, especially in the ears. Rattlesnakes were common. Rattlesnake meat was once served in the mess hall as the main dish—the first and last time for many Japanese, who felt that feeding rattlesnake was an insult, even though the Japanese dearly love eel, which is no more appetizing to the eye than snake. The more open-minded ones admitted that rattlesnake was rather tasty, but the knowledge of what it was kept them from accepting it as regular fare.

I learned much later that Judge Lance Ito, the Los Angeles County Superior Court judge who presided over the O. J. Simpson trial in 1995, was the son of Japanese immigrants who met in Heart Mountain camp. His father, James Ito, was an inmate and served as assistant superintendent of the camp's agriculture program. Appalled that the prisoners were served only canned vegetables their first year at Heart Mountain, James Ito figured out how to bring water from the Shoshone River to irrigate the desert and turn it into fertile farmland that fed the camp residents with surplus to spare, just like the land my father had tilled at Tule Lake. Inmates dug and braced a huge root cellar, big enough to drive a truck into and store vegetables through the winter, which still exists.[7] Born in Los Angeles in 1950, Judge Ito kept photographs of the camp and a painting of Heart Mountain on the walls of his courtroom to educate potential jurors about the Japanese American incarceration and its significance under the law.

As at Tule Lake, the blocks of barracks were divided into wards, and between the wards were broad open lanes known as "firebreaks." These firebreaks were designed to prevent the whole camp from going up in flames in case of fire, because tar-papered barracks with lath posed a huge fire risk. Every morning before

Me with Ma, Gene, and Dick at Heart Mountain camp; a guard tower can be seen at right, and the namesake mountain is just visible over Ma's shoulder. (Asai family collection)

school, we would go out into the firebreak and recite the Pledge of Allegiance.

In those days, girls were not allowed to wear pants, so we always wore dresses and skirts. Crossing those firebreaks on my way to and from school was sometimes painful because dust storms blew sand and winter blizzards blew snow sideways, causing me to stop, cover my legs, and cry, as I tried to get a rest from the stinging. Then I'd get up and run some more. The dust storms were worse than the snow blizzards. They were so bad that you'd close all the doors and windows, but somehow they'd get into the barracks. You could even feel the dust clinging between your teeth.

We had lots of parties and celebrations, some associated with holidays, but more of them were dances: Fourth of July, Christmas, American holidays. Japanese holidays included Boys Day, when boys could fly the nice kites, and Girls Day, when girls could decorate dolls. But there wasn't a patriotic or cultural Japanese element about those. After the segregation center was set up in Tule Lake, cultural celebrations were very much discouraged there, but I wasn't aware of that in the other nine camps.

There were classes available in the camp for almost any interest: sewing, drafting, flower arranging, tea ceremony, Japanese dance, and for the youth, sports recreation clubs. We also had Girl Scouts, Camp Fire Girls, and Y-Teens. Ma learned drafting. Whereas before, she had made clothes freehand, now she could make a pattern out of newspapers or brown paper, and then sew a dress for me with the pattern she had made.

Ma's fall down the stairs when we were packing to go to camp seemed to make her rheumatism worse. As the war years wore on, it bothered her more and more. She went to a masseur, which helped a little. I too would massage her almost every evening. Later she used a Japanese *yaito*, or "burn cure," in which skin is burned in strategic pain areas by lighting a small stick or wooden material placed on the skin. This was supposed to burn the nerve endings.

This treatment helped more than anything else.

In Heart Mountain, Ma had gall bladder surgery. A nurse in attendance said they did not have her dentures removed during surgery (common practice) because no one realized she had dentures! My sister added that the dentures fit so well that they could not be detected.

I was a happy child in camp. Before incarceration in the fourth grade, I lived on a farm and my closest neighbor was Margaret Takagi. I had to walk up the road about a quarter of a mile to play with her. Now we were all in a camp with kids everywhere, the way you'd be in a housing project. It was great: We'd go out the door and had immediate friends to play with, and nothing to do because we weren't on the farm anymore. So it was a picnic for us, whereas before we'd had drudgery on the farm.

For my older sister, it was a much bleaker experience. She was nine years older than I; she had just graduated from high school, and there wasn't much for her to do. She couldn't go to college, she couldn't get a job, she couldn't go anywhere. So for her, it was a disaster. Surely it was hard for my folks, too. But I had no idea.

With my friends Kaz Hayano (left) and Fumie Hiuga (whose brother Harold later married my sister Mika) at Heart Mountain in 1944 or '45. (Asai family collection)

Every once in a while, my father would get into a serious, contemplative state while following the news of the war. While we were in camp, the main questions in the minds of people like my parents were: Will we ever get to go home? When? How many years are we going to stay here? What will be the condition of our homes, farms, and businesses when we return? What will become of our children who grow up in these camps? Will our sons survive the war? Will they be wounded, maimed, or killed? If they should die, what will become of us, who need their help?

Some of the old folks would get together and listen to reports of the progress of the war. We were not allowed to have radios, but there must have been a contraband shortwave radio somewhere in the camp, because the Issei would gather at some hush-hush place to listen to news. Pa often came home worried from these broadcasts. He'd say something that would stop me short, and I'd be left with the impression that something serious was going on, but not really knowing or understanding what.

If the Americans were losing, he'd say the war is going badly, and if the Japanese were winning, he worried maybe his sons would be killed. Pa's comments were always the same. Shaking his head, he would speak of those "fool Japanese military leaders who think they can win a war that's impossible to win . . . those dreamers, caught up in their own visions of grandeur and might, dragging along the rest of the nation, with the same insane resultant deaths of humans on both sides."

I was having a great time with all my friends. When I've talked about the camp experience in recent years, people often say, "You always look so happy [in the photographs] and you don't seem to have any anger or anything." It's just my personality. Pa always said you should never harbor negative emotions. Anger, sadness, grief, and regret are all a waste of time. I got that from my father.

In Heart Mountain, I joined Camp Fire Girls, which enabled me to take advantage of a week's summer camping in nearby

Yellowstone Park. There I saw Old Faithful, other geysers, and many of the other natural wonders. The most vivid memory I have of that week was one night when I was awakened by a loud noise like the sound of breaking boards. We slept in a large bunkhouse in rows of beds, perhaps forty in all. There was a large door at the end of the bunkhouse with a bar across it to lock out unwanted intruders. When I rose out of my bed, I could see through the dim light some movement at the door. I walked toward the door close enough to see a large furry paw. I screamed, woke many of the others who joined in with their screams, and the paw disappeared. There was a large knothole in the door, which the bear had poked and pounded until the hole was large enough to put his paw through. That was the sound I had heard.

The next day, after we had gone for a long hike, we returned to the bunkhouse and found large muddy footprints on several of our beds. Our friend had been able to get inside after all; I was glad he had done it while we were gone. I have since had the pleasure of seeing Yellowstone twice more: once when we took our two older children on a tour of the national parks and monuments in the West in 1966, and again in 1969 when we took all three boys across the United States en route to Europe.

Christmas Comes—Even Behind Barbed Wire

Newspaper photo of a play in which I was a little angel in Heart Mountain camp. Even at age 12, I grabbed the microphone. (Asai family collection)

There were occasional "victory bond sales" throughout the war years wherein we were encouraged to buy US Government Savings Bonds to support the war effort. A huge rally was staged with music, well-known speakers, and more. On April 24, 1944, a Japanese American hero, Ben Kuroki, spoke at Heart Mountain.

Kuroki had grown up in rural Nebraska. The day after Pearl Harbor, he enlisted in the army with his brother Fred. Ben Kuroki was one of the few Japanese American men who flew warplanes during the war. He completed fifty-eight combat missions as a turret gunner in B-24 and B-29 bombers over both Europe and the Pacific. He appeared in our camp covered with war ribbons and medals. The authorities also took him to speak to people in the Minidoka camp in Idaho and Topaz in Utah.[8]

Many years later, in 1998, he recalled in a video interview, "Of course I was really quite shocked when I approached Heart Mountain and came up to the gate and saw these armed guards, and they were all wearing the same uniform I was wearing. And inside, behind the barbed wire, were all . . . my own people. Most of them, as you know, were American citizens. It was really quite a shock, and I never did get over that."[9]

From the very beginning, any adult Nisei could apply to leave the camps, and if security clearance were granted, he or she could go to school or work anywhere in the United States, so long as it was outside of the three Pacific coastal states. Later in the war, the government felt more certain of the loyalty of the Japanese, and security clearances were granted to the Issei as well. Pa left Heart Mountain to work in the sugar beet and potato fields in Montana. Later, he worked on the railroad there.

I recall little about Pa's days in Montana except that he had two old friends from Hood River who went with him, Mr. Sato and Mr. Akiyama. They slept in common quarters and shared in living expenses. There were several references and jokes made about the fact that both Pa and Mr. Akiyama snored, while Mr. Sato was fortunately a little hard of hearing. Between Pa and Mr. Akiyama, the first to go to sleep had the advantage of not having to listen to the other one snoring.

Since Ma could write very little, I cannot remember how we communicated with Pa when he was away. I believe he wrote to us in Japanese syllabary, which all of us could somehow read cooperatively. Then Ma and I scrawled a few lines in the same syllabary back to him. Brothers Gene and Dick did not bother with letters. They were busy collecting and typing up the words to popular songs of the day to put into a scrapbook.

Pa was away for months but returned to camp sooner than he wanted because of Ma's gall bladder surgery in 1944. He used to say that he wore out the soles of his shoes going to visit Ma in the hospital every day, which we thought was an exaggeration. When I visited Heart Mountain in July 2019, however, I learned that the camp was two miles square and that we lived in a barrack in the northernmost, western corner. The hospital was in the opposite northern corner to the east. So in fact he *did* walk two miles to and two miles back every day. For once, anyway, he had not teased us with an exaggeration.

Mika's strongest memory of those years was a day when Western Union called her. She went to the office and learned that Min had wired her some money from Chicago, an unexpected but welcome surprise. She also remembered that Half bought US Savings Bonds and postal savings stamps throughout his army career. She wondered where the money could have come from, after the ten-dollar deduction from his twenty-one-dollar paycheck.

Her friend Bessie, who later married brother Min, remembered most vividly that they could not go into Temple Square in Salt Lake City because they were not Mormons. A Japanese American soldier friend who was also from Hood River, Harry Tamura, came to visit Bessie and Mika, and escorted by him they were able to see Temple Square.

Mika made brief daily trips away from Heart Mountain camp to help local farmers who needed potato harvesters. Citizens and aliens worked for piecework wages, but when they found that they could not make enough money that way, the farmers agreed to pay them fifty cents an hour. Mika remembers the kindness of the farmers, who sometimes gave the workers from camp a chunk of butter or fresh eggs, and in general shared what they had. On the way to the farms, Mika stopped at a grocery store, where she saw her first wartime ration coupons, which we of course did not have to deal with in the camps. The potato harvest work lasted ten days. Mika's total earnings of fifty dollars went toward the purchase of an overcoat.

When the Japanese community of Hood River had been "evacuated" in the spring of 1942, some families were still paying large mortgages on their farms. By 1941, Pa had paid off his. From 1910 or 1911, when he bought that land up in the hills, until 1941, he had acquired two more orchards. He still owned the original property on the hillside where he had cleared timberland to start his first farm—the farm where he had delivered most of my siblings. Then there was one closer to town, near the intersection of Portland Drive and Riverdale Road. My eldest brother Tot's children farm that land to this day.

The third property, across the road from the golf course and maybe a half mile from the historic Oak Grove store, Pa acquired in a mortgage settlement from another Japanese man who had borrowed money from him. The original owner did not do well with his farm and could not pay Pa, who had to foreclose. I am guessing this would have been about 1937. It was not a good orchard—mostly old trees that needed to be replaced by younger ones that would bear enough fruit to make the farm pay. By the time the war came, Pa had taken out all the old trees, replanted, and grown the new stand just to the point of the first good harvest, when we had to leave Hood River for the camps.

My father had worked hard to raise a family of seven (not counting eldest daughter Masako, left in Japan), and when the war came, he had three orchards, no mortgages, and money in the bank. We used to tease him and say, "You're not Japanese, you're Scottish!" Most of the other farmers in the camps had mortgages, were imprisoned for three years with no income, and had no extra money in the bank. In some cases, the government just took their property. That happened more in California than in Oregon or Washington.

Pa had only to find someone to lease the properties. The neighbor to the orchard Pa had acquired through foreclosure on an unpaid loan wrote to us when we were in camp and said that the man who was leasing our farm had not sprayed or taken proper care of the orchard. This was having an adverse effect on his trees, he said, which adjoined Pa's farm. Pa was pretty sure he was lying, so he didn't answer.

Pa wrote to the man who was leasing the property and relayed the neighbor's complaint. He was not surprised to receive a letter from his lessee who said there was no foundation to the neighbor's charges. We got the impression that the neighbor was inventing trouble, but we were trapped in camp and could not investigate on our own to confirm our suspicions. Some time later, the neighbor wrote again to state that nothing had been done in response to his first complaint; do something, or I'm taking you to court. We didn't have any income and were locked up. How could we be expected to get a lawyer to fight this man?

The man added that if Pa could not satisfy him, we had better sell the property to him so that the orchard could be given proper care. We suspected greed as a motive, and this second letter seemed to confirm that. But having no sense of how long we would be detained in camp, or how to appease the neighbor with his invented charges, Pa sadly and with resignation agreed to sell the farm to him. This whole episode was the source of a great deal of bitterness and regret for Pa for many years. Pa's respect for the man diminished, and I do not believe he spoke to him the remaining twenty-five years of his life.

Heart Mountain was the site of both stiff opposition to the US draft and Nisei who would serve heroically in the war. As the Heart Mountain Wyoming Foundation website explains, "Having been forced from their homes, imprisoned, and labeled 'unfit,' many were not enthusiastic when Army recruiters came . . . in the spring of 1943. Only 38 volunteered."[10]

The government reactivated the draft for Nisei men in January 1944, and the Heart Mountain Fair Play Committee organized to protest. About eight hundred Nisei renounced their US citizenship, and hospital workers staged a five-day strike.[11] Eventually, a total of sixty-three Heart Mountain resisters were convicted of violations of the Selective Service Act and sentenced to three to five years in federal prison.[12] President Truman pardoned them all in 1947, but many in the Japanese American community continued to regard them as traitors and cowards, rather than American citizens who had stood up for their rights against a government that had wronged them.

In all, 385 men were inducted straight out of the camp, and more than 800 from Heart Mountain, both volunteers and draftees, would leave to serve in the armed forces.[13] Fifteen would be killed in action,[14] and fifty-two wounded in combat.[15] Two Nisei servicemen with families at Heart Mountain, Joe Hayashi (who had volunteered in Los Angeles in May 1941[16]) and James K. Okubo, posthumously received the Medal of Honor for valor in battle.[17] This made Heart Mountain the only one of the ten camps that could boast of more than one such honoree.[18]

When Americans hear about Japanese American soldiers, many picture the 442nd Combat Team, which is famous for being the most decorated unit in US military history. Formed in the spring of 1943, when the war was already half over, it was composed almost entirely of Japanese American citizens, to show the rest of the American people that "we're not only loyal, we're brave fighters, and can do better than anybody else." That regiment fought in the European Theater—in Italy, southern France, and Germany.

When people find out both my brothers went overseas but served in the Pacific Theater, they're surprised. But why? If the United States were at war with Sweden, Americans of Swedish descent would still fight the Swedes while serving in the US Army, right? As I write this, Russians and Russian speakers who live in Ukraine are fighting Russian soldiers they regard as invaders.

While we were in Heart Mountain, Half was given his month's furlough before going overseas. He came to visit us. After a few days "home," he left without saying anything to anyone. Ma wept, both from worry over his whereabouts and sadness at his disappearance. Some days later, he sent a letter apologizing for his sudden departure. He admitted that he could not bear the indignity of spending his leave time in a camp where his parents and family were locked up while he was serving in the US Army.

While we were fighting insects in Wyoming, my eldest brother, Tot, was doing the same in Bougainville, in the Solomon Islands, and other South Pacific locations. He served with the 37th Infantry, the Ohio Buckeye Division. Much later, one of his Hood River buddies, Mam Noji, recalled something my oldest brother had said as they left San Francisco Bay for the Pacific Theater: "When Tot and I were going underneath the Golden Gate Bridge, he says, 'I figure that we've only got a fifty-fifty chance of seeing that bridge again.' Until then I never thought of not coming back. Fifty-fifty's not good odds, is it?"

Tot's assignment in the army was with the Military Intelligence Service (MIS). He attended the MIS language school in Fort Snelling, Minnesota, to hone his Japanese speaking and writing skills and to master Japanese military terms. On duty in the Pacific, he worked as an interpreter and translator. Sometimes his task was to go unarmed into the nearby hills and caves around the US Army encampment at a battle's end. He would search for civilians and soldiers who were hiding, huddled together and fearful of the worst from the American enemy.

It was my brother's job to talk to them and coax them to come out and give themselves up, rather than commit suicide or die of exposure or starvation. The insignia of the Ohio Buckeye Division was a red circle on a white background. When the Japanese saw this on Tot's shoulder, they were mighty confused because it closely resembled the rising sun emblem of Japan. This, coupled with a Japanese face on an apparent American soldier who spoke Japanese, was a lot for them to sort out. He would talk to them awhile before Red Cross trucks were sent in. Any apprehension they might have shown before this quickly disappeared when they saw the Red Cross logo, and they readily gave themselves up.

Sgt. Taro Asai interrogates two Japanese prisoners of war captured by the 129th Infantry Regiment near Trinidad, Luzon, the Philippines. (Photo from the National Archive, credited to T/5 Stettner, May 2, 1945)

Tot eventually contracted a fungus infection called "jungle rot," the size of a silver dollar as he described it, on his neck. He was sent to New Caledonia for six months to be cured. It would not heal because of the humid climate, so he was returned to his unit. He suffered from this infection the rest of his life, especially when he perspired a great deal in the heat of summer. Tot noted that when he sprayed the fruit trees with fungicide, if some of the spray hit his neck fungus, it had a soothing effect.

My brother remembered stopping ten to fourteen days in Fiji while en route to Guadalcanal, New Hebrides, and Bougainville. Gas was rationed in the States, but it was plentiful in Guadalcanal, Tot said. Later he went to Baguio City, Luzon, on the northern island of the Philippines, after passing through New Guinea in a "pincer movement" with US Marines from the south and the army from the north. There was not much fighting in New Guinea, but the Baguio area was occupied by both US and Japanese troops— about half and half. Tot described the Japanese Army's equipment as "of Civil War vintage." But, he commented, they had beautiful vegetable gardens, which the US Army tried to destroy because they were the enemy's food supply.

He had his army fatigue uniform on when he arrived, and the marines, not recognizing the US Army uniform, yelled, "Let's get these Japs!" Someone said, "What's the matter with you guys? Can't you see he has on a US uniform?" Their reply was, "He's a Jap. He stole the uniform." Tot was not harmed, but he was plenty frightened.

When the United States dropped atomic bombs on Hiroshima and Nagasaki, two of my brothers were in the Pacific Theater with their respective army units, so I do not know how they felt about it. I do recall that Pa felt very bad about it. No one, including Pa, understood the significance of this new weapon, but the best word to describe his feelings then was "grave."

He never actually talked against it, although I'm sure he felt that it was a terrible mistake on the part of the United States. He had a generally high regard for Truman and his decisions (which included the president's firing of General MacArthur), but in this case, he thought that Truman acted unwisely on the suggestion of his advisors. Military necessity or expediency did not justify such an action in his mind or the minds of many Americans then and since.

As for the rest of us, our reactions were similar to that of most Americans. We did not understand the import or the power of this new scientific means of destruction. There was a sort of bewilderment connected with any thought of the atom bomb. It is strange to remember that we felt this way, in view of the relative nonchalance with which present-day Americans react to missiles, hydrogen bombs, and other descendants of atomic weaponry.

When I went to Japan as a goodwill ambassador with the Fulbright program in 1957 and 1958, I questioned many people about how they felt regarding the bomb. My host's response to my question was: "All's fair in war. War is war. We started the war, and we had to expect the worst." Under further questioning, however, beyond the polite preliminaries, I sensed that deep down he felt as Pa did.

My eldest brother's experience in the South Pacific further exemplified the "war is hell" feeling of the time. There was in Tot's army unit a young boy who had lied about his age in order to get into the armed services at age 17. During the heaviest fighting, their unit was instructed to go out and gather prisoners but not to kill any enemy soldiers or civilians.

This young soldier eventually found himself far away from his encampment, alone with about ten prisoners. As he shakily marched them at gunpoint back toward camp, he became more and more frightened, outnumbered as he was, despite their being unarmed. His youth did not stand the test of such pressure in this situation. He lined them up against a fence in front of a ditch beside the road and shot them, letting their bodies fall down into the ditch. He then returned to camp.

My brother slept in the next bunk to this boy and noticed that he was extremely disturbed, nervous, and fitful in his sleep. He would scream and toss at night, plagued with the memory of his actions and the subsequent nightmares and sick conscience. Often he would wake sobbing, and my brother would sit up with him and try to console him. What was bothering him? The boy finally broke down and told my brother everything.

All the soldiers in his unit eventually learned the whole story, but none reported it. If they had, he would have been court-martialed for disobeying orders. They all realized this soldier's situation might very well have been their own. A discreet silence was kept about the whole thing. Perhaps the officers heard the story too, but nothing came of it. I have wondered how the Japanese could have (and may very well have) used this episode as an example of American atrocities, had they come by the ditch and found the ten bodies lying in a row in a mass grave.

For several years thereafter, my brother would stop in the middle of some dinner or holiday gathering and say, "I wonder what ever happened to old ____? I wonder if he's in a mental institution somewhere." This was greeted by silence and a momentary suspension of the gay and happy atmosphere that reigned previous to his remark.

More than forty years after the war ended, Tot and his wife Marie made a trip to Australia and stopped to see Tot's familiar World War II spots in Fiji.

CHAPTER 10

We Go Home at Last

On December 18, 1944, the US Supreme Court ruled a third time, in *Korematsu v. U.S.*, that the "evacuation" was a "military necessity" to protect against espionage from Japan, and that it had not been based on racism.[1] But the vote was 6-3, and in a strongly worded dissent, Justice Robert Jackson wrote that in trying to avoid being sent to the camps, Fred Korematsu "has been convicted of an act not commonly thought a crime. It consists merely of being present in the state whereof he is a citizen, near the place where he was born, and where all his life he has lived." Justice Frank Murphy, a fellow dissenter, asserted the exclusion "falls into the ugly abyss of racism" and resembled "the abhorrent and despicable treatment of minority groups by the dictatorial tyrannies which this nation is now pledged to destroy."[2]

The same day, in *Ex parte Mitsuye Endo*, the justices issued a unanimous ruling that the government could not continue to hold a citizen who was "concededly loyal" to the United States. Like me, Ms. Endo—who was employed by the California Department of Motor Vehicles in Sacramento before the war, was born in this country, and a Christian—had a brother in the US Army. The War Relocation Authority did not have the power, the opinion by Justice William O. Douglas stated, "to detain citizens against whom no charges of disloyalty or subversiveness have been made for a period longer than that necessary to separate the loyal from the disloyal."[3]

Together, the two rulings don't make a lot of sense, especially since Douglas's opinion in *Endo* dodged the issue of the constitutionality of the camps. But the ruling in the second case seemed to indicate imprisonment was illegal for at least the two-thirds of us who were American citizens. Warned in advance of the decisions, President Roosevelt's administration rescinded the exclusion orders the day before,[4] and declared Japanese Americans could begin returning home in January 1945.

A probable underlying factor in this move was the sheer expense of the incarceration program. The WRA's budget over those three or four years amounted to $162 million, and the army spent an additional $75 million on rounding up and transporting us.[5] Part of that money came out of our own pockets, in the form of the federal taxes we were paying.

A beaming Dick and somber Ma board the bus in camp for Hood River, April 1945. (Asai family collection)

The Supreme Court ruling was cause for rejoicing among Japanese Americans, but many of the "folks back home" were not so pleased. In California, fruit packing sheds owned by Japanese Americans were dynamited. Shots were fired at farmhouses from cars speeding by at night. Telephone threats came from anonymous callers. Unexplained fires and a few beatings occurred.

My brother Min, then working in Chicago, applied to the government for permission to return to Hood River, which was still in the war-restricted zone. He asked that the ban be lifted for him. With two friends, Ray Sato and Sat Noji, Min wanted to make sure it was safe before having any families return to town. Sato returned from Cleveland, where he had been working in a war plant. The three would be the first Japanese Americans to survey the situation in Hood River.

In a January 1943 newspaper poll, supposedly of a cross-section of Hood River County, a disturbing 84 percent of the 352 residents questioned said they did not want Japanese to return to the valley after the war; 9 percent would accept only US citizens, 5 percent were favorable to our return, and only 2 percent were undecided.[6] By early 1945, a local American Legion member had told the *Oregonian*: "There is a high feeling against them. There will be violence."[7] Expected to arrive on January 9, 1945, Ray, Sat, and Min were not aboard the train for which a "reception committee" waited. Instead, they arrived on Friday, January 12.

A small story on the front page of the *Oregonian* the following day reported the three men's arrival in Hood River at 5:40 a.m. to what the paper characterized as "utter calm, in contrast to the recent fury of opposition publicity spearheaded by the American Legion post here"[8] (about which you'll hear considerably more in a moment). The three were met at the train station by Clyde Linville, the War Relocation Authority agent from Portland, who drove them to Sato's home seventeen miles south of town. Min had to depend on Carl and Hazel Smith, our good neighbors, for a place to live until our house was vacated by the people who had leased our orchard.

Linville drove seventy miles every day from Portland to check on the young men's well-being. Among his services was to pressure Standard Oil's head office to compel local fuel delivery to our farms, so the three returnees could maintain a beachhead in their hometown. Linville became a personal friend of many in Hood River and continued to live in Oregon, eventually moving to Hood River in his retirement years. My brother Min named his second son Carl Clyde, after Carl Smith and Clyde Linville.

When it appeared no store in town would sell to them, a sympathetic orchardist from the upper valley, Avon Sutton, braved the ostracism of his neighbors to purchase and deliver the provisions the young men needed.

Sato once walked into a bank in town, and Doris Burgoyne, a bank employee and wife of the new Methodist minister in town, left her desk to shake his hand. Thereafter she was treated so coldly by her coworkers that she eventually quit her job.[9] Regulars outside the pool hall stared and spat. "What the hell are you doing here?" one man yelled at Min. "I live here," my brother replied. "Well, why don't you go back where you're from?" the man yelled. "But I'm from here," Min said. "I was born here."[10]

To save time, trouble, and embarrassment, Min wrote a letter and sent copies of it to many local businesses to ask if Japanese customers would be welcome in these establishments.

Hazel Smith's cousin, Ralph Sherrieb—the man who had given us an address book in tears three years before—owned a general store about a mile from her home. Now he had a "No Jap Trade" sign on the door of his store. One day Ralph confronted his cousin Hazel in the store and declared, "I don't like the way you are handling the Jap situation." Hazel replied, "You mean you don't approve of my having Min Asai as a houseguest? I suppose you don't want me to be seen trading in your store. Well, I don't care to!" She walked out and never stepped into her cousin's store again.

As far as I know, Hazel Smith had no future association with her cousin Ralph. He died in the 1960s after retiring and moving to set up a roadside fruit stand outside Coos Bay, where my own family would settle in 1971. Ralph named it Hood River Fruit, a landmark for many decades on the Cape Arago Highway just a few miles from where my boys grew up.

Carl and Hazel Smith retired from the fruit orchard and lived their last days in Portland, where Hazel passed away in 1986. The Smiths live on in the grateful memories of many Japanese Americans in Hood River, who can never forget the courage and kindness of these gentle folk. An interesting update is that my nephew, Sam Asai, oldest son of my brother Min, lived in the old Smith house with his family for a time. He moved there in the 1980s from Portland, after he quit working as an accountant and decided to be a fruit farmer instead. He and his family eventually settled on their own orchard in Oak Grove two or three miles from the old Smith farm.

Sat Noji's sister and parents were the first family with Nisei serving in the military to return to Hood River. Aside from Clyde Linville's daily visits, they were buoyed by the consideration of their farm's caretaker, R. J. McIsaac, who owned a general store in Parkdale up the valley. He took good care of their orchard while they were in camp, kept meticulous records, and supplied them with accurate financial returns.

When our house was finally vacated, Min moved in alone and was soon joined by a stray dog, which he named "Friend." This dog is mentioned in one of the Department of Interior War Relocation Authority official reports of 1946, although Min is not identified by name in the report.

Min was short of wood to burn in the stove, so he cut down an old cherry tree that stood next to the house. He then dried a few pieces at a time in the oven—enough that they would burn in the old kitchen stove that was still in use in the house and would continue to be for many years. Back in the days when I was learning how to cook, I had used this same stove.

Min had intended to run the farm alone for the time being, but as soon as he returned home, the Selective Service Board changed his draft classification from 4-C (unfit for service) to 1-A (top class to be inducted). He remarked later that his loyalty to the United States had not changed in the eyes of the board; they just wanted him out of the Hood River Valley.

Min called Pa and told him that the family should come home right away, if it were Pa's intention to leave the camp, because Min was sure that he would be drafted into the service shortly—and he was right. Min passed the physical examination and served in the army from June 1945 to 1947. The board also changed the draft classification for his two buddies, but one had flat feet and the other had heart trouble, so they were not compelled to leave town.

Before my brother joined his two siblings in the service, the local American Legion post sent agents to try to buy the Asai orchard from him. In July 1981, when hearings on potential reparations for the incarceration of Japanese Americans during the war opened in Washington, DC, Min told a reporter for the *New York Times*: "I ran them off. The powers around here thought that if they could stop us three, the others would not come back."[11]

The week that the government announced we could return to Oregon, there was much excitement in our family as well as the other families in the camps. Some Japanese had already returned to their homes in California and been greeted with vandalism, vigilantism, theft, and intimidation. Our hometown weekly newspaper, the *Hood River News*, had printed full-page paid ads every week in the months of January, February, and March 1945, warning the Japanese not to return. "You are not wanted," they said. "If you come back, we will make life miserable for you." They were serious, as we were to learn from personal experience.

The self-appointed chairman of the anti-Japanese committee, Kent Shoemaker, supported by the local American Legion Post No. 22, sought to "keep the Japs from returning to this county." Shoemaker had been active in this way for a long time. As reported in a brief news story in the October 23, 1919, issue of the *Oregonian* (twenty-six years earlier, but fifteen years after my father's arrival in this country), Shoemaker was president of the Hood River post of the American Legion and championed a resolution proposed by local orchardists to "forward an anti-Japanese resolution" in "opposition to Asiatic ownership of land."[12]

Each of the full-page ads in 1945 contained a short letter or statement from Shoemaker on a theme such as "Only good Jap is a dead one," or "Once a Jap, always a Jap," or "So sorry, Japs are not wanted in Hood River." In one of the ads, he used the expression "Japes," a word coined by the Portland *Oregonian* newspaper that combined the two words "Jap" and "apes." Shoemaker's opening statement was followed by a petition signed by residents of Hood River County, many of whom we had known all our lives as old friends or at least acquaintances.

Many names were unfamiliar, though. These were people who had never known us but had moved to Hood River during the war—perhaps after working in the Portland shipyards—and who had decided to stay in Oregon. It was bewildering and discouraging, to say the least, to peruse these columns of names each week and see which of our old friends had succumbed to the petition. After seven weeks of such ads, there was hardly anybody left, which we found discouraging.

But we learned whom we could call upon for help. There are people who will always stand up for the right, and possibly suffer for it. "A friend in need is a friend indeed" came to have real meaning to us. I can name the eight or so families who were our champions to this day because that's how important they were to us. Of course, Carl and Hazel Smith's names could not be found in those newspaper ads under the petition. And not Max Moore, Don Yeck, Fred Taylor, Sherman Burgoyne, Avon Sutton, Elmer Moller, or the Hoerleins. They formed the League for Liberty and Justice to combat the activities of such men as Mr. Shoemaker, C. A. Perkins, George Frey, and Jess Edington, commander of the American Legion post. The good league took its name from the final words of the Pledge of Allegiance: "and liberty and justice for all."

More was required of people in the way of moral courage and humanity than many could stand. These people suffered the same as we did. Some of the hardware stores wouldn't do business with members of the League for Liberty and Justice because of their support for us.

Mrs. Max Moore, owner of an electrical store in town, and the Reverend Burgoyne of the Asbury Methodist Church were to be of great assistance during the especially trying times that followed, when befriending the returning Japanese was no way to gain popularity. The Reverend Burgoyne, said to be a descendant of the British General John Burgoyne defeated by General Horatio Gates in the Revolutionary War Battle of Saratoga in 1777, had been born in Montana in 1901 and came to Oregon in 1928.[13] He and his wife Doris arrived in Hood River in the summer of 1942 after we had all been sent away, and reportedly had never met a Japanese American up to that point. But the honor roll incident, which I will relate shortly, would bring the Reverend Burgoyne national attention and broad local notoriety.

Frozen out of membership in civic clubs and unable to find any buyers for his pear crop, the Reverend Burgoyne was forced to sell his ten-acre farm with the fruit still unpicked on the trees. After the Mollers once invited Tot to dinner, the Elks Club blackballed Elmer Moller. "I've had Elks to dinner too," he snapped. Frances

Moller, a tall, loud-voiced neighbor, who had been a teacher in Odell, was known for her blunt, direct ways. Having done house-cleaning for her, I had firsthand experience with Mrs. Moller. I once called her on the telephone, and before I could say anything, she shouted into the phone, "I'm making butter right now; it's on the stove. Call me later." *Slam!* went the receiver as I stood aston-ished, holding the receiver at my end in midair.

C. A. Perkins, a local wholesaler active in the local American Legion post, hired some high school boys to drive through the Ogawa property late at night to frighten the female residents (Mrs. Ogawa, a widow, and her two daughters were farming while the son and brother Masao was in the US Army). Later, Mrs. Moller, who knew Mr. Perkins well, stopped him on the street in Hood River. In her loudest voice, intended to reach the ears of all pass-ersby, she said, "Why, Mr. Perkins, you big hunk of a man! You're getting handsomer every day. And to think, a big hunk of a man like you would stoop so low as to frighten a poor widow and her daughters!" Mrs. Moller then walked away, leaving a red-faced Mr. Perkins standing on the street before the eyes of a number of per-plexed passersby. Only Mr. Perkins and Mrs. Moller understood what it was all about.

On other occasions, Mrs. Moller was known to go into stores that bore a "No Jap Trade" sign. She would pick up one small in-expensive item, and just before paying for it, she would say, "Oh, I see that you a have a 'No Jap Trade' sign in your window. My maiden name is Oberteuffer. That's German, you know. Does that matter? Will you sell it to me?" The poor innocent clerk was bewil-dered by all this—an act Mrs. Moller always put on in front of as many store customers as she could catch for her audience.

There were only four of our family left at Heart Mountain. According to camp records, Mika left for Salt Lake City on January 25, 1944, and after Gene graduated from high school in the camp, he left on August 2, 1944—initially to Payette, Idaho, and then

Cleveland, Ohio, for work.[14] When Pa asked if we wanted to go home, Dick and I said yes, but Ma said no. Her fears had been fed by the content of the newspapers, which others had explained to her. My dad eventually decided that we would return, my mother being outvoted 3-1. He did suggest that she could stay in the camp if she wanted. Of course, my mother came with us.

There's a photo of Dick and me excitedly standing at a bus or train station near Heart Mountain, when we were about to leave camp to go home. He's going to be in high school, and I'm going to be in my final year of elementary school—the seventh grade. The sign above us says "Vocation Heart Mountain." I don't recall how long it took to travel by bus from Wyoming to Oregon. Each of us got twenty-five dollars to start life over after three years: a hundred dollars total for our family of four.

The Asai family arrived in Hood River on April 20, 1945. We were a "test" family in our community. Many other Japanese families waited to see how we fared before deciding whether to come back. I remember the day well because it was snowing as our train pulled into the station, very unusual weather. The snow and cold weather seemed to foreshadow the cold reception we would receive from our hometown in the days to come.

I was especially eager on the day of our return to see the local "honor roll" of servicemen, which was mounted on the outside wall of the County Courthouse. There was an honor roll like it in almost every US town during the war. The one in Hood River measured 100 × 20 feet, listed sixteen hundred names, and included the names of sixteen Japanese American boys in 1944, two of them being my brothers Tot and Half. On November 28, 1944, a commercial painter hired by the local American Legion Post No. 22 used white paint to blank out those sixteen names from the honor roll.[15] (The name of an additional Nisei boy from the county, Isao Namba, was mistaken for Finnish and not effaced.)[16]

The Honor Roll on the Hood River county courthouse, 1945 (Ralph Vincent, the History Museum, Hood River)

Various individuals and organizations across the state and the nation were quick to condemn the action. By that Saturday, December 2, the Portland Council of Churches and Roger Baldwin, director of the American Civil Liberties Union, had spoken out.[17] The Hood River Legion post responded the following Monday. It asserted that any Japanese person born in the United States was also registered in Japan, and the Japanese government paid twenty-five dollars to the parents of any boy born here. "The alien and American-born Japanese are being infiltrated back to the Pacific coast against the wishes of a majority of the residents . . . thereby endangering our military operations, enhancing the danger of riot, destruction of property and the peace and good order in these communities."[18]

Throughout the ensuing weeks, the dispute was often front-page news in the *Oregonian*, Portland's daily newspaper, as well as in its letters columns inside. By mid-December, multiple American Legion posts across the nation had protested the defacement of the honor roll in Hood River. The Capt. Belvidere Brooks legion post in New York City voted unanimously to invite the sixteen Hood River Nisei veterans to join their post after the war.[19]

Robert D. Cozzens—assistant director of the War Relocation Authority, a World War I veteran, and member of the American Legion—said the Hood River post had "betrayed the Legion by a deliberate insult to our army," and added, "I know that your disgraceful act cannot be condoned by a vast majority of American Legionnaires, nor by the lost battalion rescued in this war by Nisei [in Europe]." President Roosevelt's secretary of war, Henry Stimson, told the press it was not consistent with democratic ideals "that these loyal citizens should be subjected to discrimination," and he praised the fighting spirit of Japanese American soldiers.[20]

Ironically, on December 16, the *Oregonian* reported that one of the sixteen Hood River servicemen, Private Eichi Wakamatsu, had been wounded in action in France on October 30. His parents received the news at Granada "relocation center," also known as Camp Amache, in Colorado where they were imprisoned.[21] The news report also noted that two Japanese American soldiers from Gresham, privates George M. Hata and Hiromu Heyamoto, had been wounded in Italy and France, respectively, earlier in the year. Parents of both servicemen were being held in Minidoka camp, in south central Idaho. Also, although we wouldn't learn this until later, my brother Half's good friend Frank Hachiya had been killed in action that same winter in Leyte. His name had not been on the honor roll because he had not registered for the draft in Hood River.

The local American Legion post continued to hold the line. On December 19, it issued another public statement, which claimed "we have every good reason to believe [the honor roll names that were removed] are citizens of Japan while claiming citizenship in this country." It demanded "an authenticated written statement that they have renounced their Japanese citizenship" and added,

"We have reason to believe that every Japanese child born in this country is registered as a citizen and subject to the call of the emperor of Japan." In a rebuke to Baldwin and the American Civil Liberties Union, the statement declared, "We on the west coast would not have the effrontery to tell the people of the east coast how they should handle or settle their race problem." It concluded: "If this is un-American or a violation of anybody's rights under the constitution of the United States, we plead guilty. This is our America and we love it."[22]

Technically, the legionnaires were at least partly right. As Linda Tamura wrote in her 2012 book about Hood River's Nisei soldiers, prior to 1924, children of Japanese citizens automatically became subjects of Japan.[23] So Nisei born before 1924 (which included Tot and Min) could indeed have taken advantage of dual citizenship, but none of us knew this or cared.

The Reverend Burgoyne swung to our defense. "It was an un-American thing to do," he said of the removal of the names. "I would have protested as loudly if the names of Jews, Negroes, Catholics, or any other group had been removed." His wife Doris's brother would be killed by a Japanese sniper on Guadalcanal, but the Burgoynes could still grasp the distinction between Issei and Nisei in the United States and Japanese imperial troops that was not apparent to the American Legion post. "My brother died to secure 'liberty and justice for all,'" Doris Burgoyne declared.

On January 5, 1945, the Reverend Burgoyne's letter to the editor appeared in the *Hood River News*. "I have tried to keep silent, seeking to persuade myself that the removing of the American service men's names was a Legion affair," he wrote. During visits to other cities, however, he said he was given the cold shoulder: "Oh! You are from That Legion town." One man asked him "if we had pushed the tombstones over in the Japanese cemetery yet!" Burgoyne declared, "every person in Hood River county . . . is disgraced." Since the courthouse belongs to the county and all its residents, he went on, "I propose that the Hood River post of the Legion take their names up on the hill to their own building and scratch off all the names they wish."[24]

By February, the national commander of the American Legion, Edward N. Scheiberling, had requested Post 22 restore the blanked names. "The action of your post has brought much unfavorable publicity and criticism to the American Legion," his telegram read. "I therefore recommend that the Hood River post reconsider its action and restore the names removed from the honor roll."[25] Letters to the editor in the *Oregonian*,

Arline Moore (Mrs. Max Moore) and the Reverend Sherman Burgoyne examine the names on the honor roll. (Homer Yasui, June 16, 1946)

especially from active service members and military chaplains who had served in Europe and the Pacific, largely supported the Nisei soldiers, as did two-thirds of the nearly four hundred letters sent directly to Post 22 by active-duty soldiers, veterans, ministers, and other private citizens.

But Hood River Post 22 and commander Shoemaker dug in their heels and published six full-page ads in the newspaper[26] to "preserve Hood River for the standard way of living," always closing with "Yours for a Hood River without a Jap." These were the ads that had so frightened and discouraged Ma.

Opposition to the action by the Hood River post was not universal. In a letter to the *Oregonian*, one Portland resident claimed, "A Jap can never aspire to civilization and culture as we know it."[27] A spokesman for the Remember Pearl Harbor League in Kent, Washington, stated that his organization would redouble its efforts to prevent the return of Japanese and urged local farmers to unite against the sale or lease of land to them.[28] The mayor of Vancouver, British Columbia, said, "I think it will be better both for their sakes and ours if they are all shipped back to Japan." Newspaper editorials in Pendleton, Pasadena, and Iowa supported Hood River post,[29] and eight other Legion posts removed Nisei names from their honor rolls as well.[30]

Perhaps most gratifying is the fact that before the controversy ended, more than three hundred servicemen in the Pacific like Tot and Half wrote letters to the *Hood River News*, and all but one criticized the local American Legion post. The news about our hometown had spread even to the far side of the globe. Mamoru Noji, one of the sixteen, overheard his Military Intelligence Service buddies in the South Pacific whisper sympathetically, "One of them guys is from Hood River."[31] Three non-Nisei servicemen from Hood River even requested their names be removed from the honor roll unless the Nisei names were replaced.[32]

Further negative publicity across the United States and pressure from the national American Legion finally convinced Hood River Post No. 22 to restore the sixteen names, but mainly because the national American Legion threatened the local post with the loss of its charter if it didn't. The names returned to the honor roll on April 9, 1945,[33] less than two weeks before we came home. Frank Hachiya's name was included this time. More than a year later, Hood River post commander Jess Edington would tell the *Oregonian* he was tired of the issue and did not want to talk about it, but he was still not ashamed of the initial step. "We just couldn't oppose the whole USA," he said.[34]

As I looked up at the honor roll on April 20, 1945, I spied the names of my two brothers. The original names had been so effectively defaced that they could not be repainted in the same spot. Consequently, the legionnaires had to put nails and hooks in those places and hang pieces of board with the names painted on them over their original spots on the honor roll. Thereafter, the Japanese American boys' names stood out from all the rest.

A few years later, my brother Tot remarked wryly that he had learned the news when he reached Manila and got his first paper after weeks in the Solomon Islands with no information from the outside world. On the front page of the *Stars and Stripes*, he read that his name had been removed from the honor roll in Hood River. "That was great for my morale," he said sarcastically.

Tot was more diplomatic when he came home and was quoted by Clarence W. Hall, editor of *The Link* and *The Chaplain*, publications of the Service Men's Christian League.[35] Asked about the honor roll incident in October 1945, he said, "I don't think the action represents the real feeling of the American people about us." With regard to how his fellow soldiers treated him in the Pacific Theater, Tot commented: "Not once did I find the slightest resentment on the part of the GIs. Always it was the highest praise and appreciation" (which might not have been strictly true but was an appropriate statement to make to the press at that point). During the initial years after the war, no Nisei veterans were allowed to join the local American Legion post, so Tot became the first Nisei vet to enroll with the Veterans of Foreign Wars in 1947, although that took several months of heated debate, a blackballing, and the resignation of some who opposed the move, before Tot was admitted to Post No. 1479.

Once we were resettled on our farm, Dick, who was barely able to reach the accelerator or old enough to get a license, drove the family vehicles, including the truck to haul fruit from the orchard to downtown Hood River to the packing houses, warehouses, and canneries run by the Apple Growers' Association. Being young, short, and Japanese, he was repeatedly pushed out of line as he waited to have his fruit unloaded or waited his turn to get a load of empty boxes to take back to the orchard. When we needed fertilizer or spray, we sometimes had to make an extra trip, because after Dick had waited in line and been pushed out, the supplier occasionally ran out before my brother got to him.

Dick and I often had to drive sixteen miles up the Hood River Valley to Parkdale, or even along the Columbia River to The Dalles or Portland (twenty-three and seventy miles, respectively), for emergency tools or mechanic help well up to his graduation in 1946-47. Our oil company stopped service abruptly without warning or explanation. Without Standard Oil's service, our desperate need for gasoline for the tractors meant that something needed to be done in a hurry. We loaded a fifty-gallon drum on the truck. Dick drove sixteen miles to R. J. McIsaac's store in Parkdale to fill the drum. Mr. McIsaac had assured us that he would do business with us. Within a week, WRA officials had looked into the situation and put things back in order, and there was no further need to drive to Parkdale for gas.

As other Nisei farmers returned to the Hood River Valley, vigilantes vandalized their equipment, broke windows, and either ostracized Japanese immigrants and Japanese Americans or prevented them from entering downtown businesses such as stores, restaurants, and movie theaters. Someone killed the Akiyamas' chickens and shot holes in their spray machines; also, the people who were supposed to take care of their farm while they were away took all the family's belongings and hung dripping bacon in their home, which left a permanent, acrid smell in the soaked floors. George Akiyama, another one of the sixteen whose names had been removed from the honor roll, had been decorated with a Silver Star, but when he sought a haircut in Hood River in 1945, he was chased out of the shop by a razor-wielding barber who said, "I ought to slit your throat."[36]

In those early years of resettling in Hood River in 1945-46, I recall the occasion of a man coming to our door to ask for help. We didn't know him; maybe he moved to Hood River during the war. But he was well known to us as unfriendly, even ugly, toward all Japanese in the valley. His vehicle had gotten stuck in the mud down the road from our house, and he knew that we were one of the few families who owned a Caterpillar tractor. Knowing that the more commonly owned rubber-tired John Deere tractors could not do the job of pulling anything out of the deep mud, he had to eat humble pie and ask us for help.

My father was rather surprised to see this man at his door, but he asked, "What can I do for you?" The man told him of his predicament. Pa said, "Let's go down there and look at the situation." Together they walked down to the place where the vehicle was mired. I have always wondered why I did not ask my father whether he had a conversation with this man as they walked together. When my father saw what had happened, he looked at the tire stuck deep in the mud, then looked at the owner and said, "It's almost to China!" Again, I wish I had asked my father if the man laughed at this point. If he didn't, he should have. They returned to our home to get the Caterpillar tractor, pulled the car out, and the episode ended. I don't know if the man ever came back to the house, sent a thank-you note, or spoke to my father anywhere in public after this.

During harvest time, our tractor stopped running. The magneto needed repair. Ormand Hukari, a man of middle age who had once begged Pa to hire him to pick strawberries (when Ormand was 6 years old) now owned a service station. Attached to the service station was a machine shop called Windmaster's, where Pa said we could take the magneto to be repaired. Dick and I took the tractor part and went to see Ormand.

Mr. Hukari said that the machine shop was leased to someone else, and he was sure that the mechanic in the shop would not do business with us. In order to help us, Ormand suggested that we come back that night after dark, hide the magneto under a shrub in front of his service station, and he would get the mechanic to work on it. We returned to the station the next night, hoping to find the magneto repaired and placed under the same shrub. We had to come back again another night before we could retrieve the magneto and get the tractor going again so the harvest could proceed. We were in such desperate need that we stooped to such actions, sneaking around in the dark like thieves. As I look back on such incidents, they seem silly and childish. It's kind of funny now, but it was pretty serious then.

I don't know for certain when all the "No Jap Trade" signs finally disappeared from store windows in Hood River, but I recall a sign or two still up by the time I graduated from the high school in 1950.

In those postwar years of resettlement in Hood River, it took me a long time to understand the pain Pa experienced over the orchard he had been forced to sell while we were in the camps. Like so many things in our family that involved deep feelings, the clarity of it all became evident only years later. With the exception of the farm tractor, Pa did not drive another vehicle after the war. He left that up to the young people.

On Sundays, Dick would take us for a Sunday drive. Every time we asked Pa to come along, he would question us thoroughly as to where we were planning to go. My brother and I would say, "Let's go for a drive!" My dad would ask, "Where are you going?" And my brother would say, "It's a Sunday drive. We don't know where we're going; we're just gonna drive around." Pa would usually say, "Well, I think I'll stay home." Once or twice, I remember that he asked if we would be driving past the country club. I know now that he would not join us because of the pain of seeing those trees he had replanted ten or twelve years before in the orchard across the road from the golf course. He had been forced to sell because a man who coveted them said, "Do something about your property which is not being properly cared for."

My brother Dick was the first Japanese American to reenter Hood River High School. On his first day of school, he was called into the office of the principal, Mr. T. A. Wells. Dick was asked not to participate in any interscholastic athletics so as not to cause any embarrassment or awkwardness. *To whom?* thought Dick. He agreed to cooperate, in spite of the fact that he was generally athletic and interested in sports. He contented himself with merely participating in intramural sports, and graduated in January 1946 after having skipped years and fulfilled his requirements by the middle of his senior year.

Mika was working as a secretary in Portland, but Pa called her home to help us on the farm. She spent a year or more at home until she was married in the fall of 1946. An old high school acquaintance who was studying for the ministry was concerned about the discrimination in Hood River. He asked Mika if she wanted to go with him to the movies to "test out" the movie theater. She did. They were refused admittance even though her date was not Japanese.

Mika recalled some prejudice against her in the prewar years. For example, she was not invited into the honor society, although other students with academic records equal to hers were voted in. There was no thought of interracial dating. Her memory of the Rotary Club was that they were "all right," but the Elks Club was definitely not cordial to Japanese before or after the war. Brother Gene married in 1953 but had to go to Washington State to do so because of Oregon laws against "mixed marriage." His wife, Barbara Jackson of Brownsville, was Caucasian. It took several more years for Oregon to remove this miscegenation law.

You might recall that in 1941, my sister Mika had worked as a live-in housekeeper for the Robert Sche family, who owned a jewelry store and lived in town. In 1945, Mika received an engagement ring that was too big. She wrote to the Sches to ask about having the ring sized. Their answer was, "Don't bring it to town. Mail it and we'll fix it and mail it back to you." This was a typical experience for us many times in the years after the war. Old friends and acquaintances wanted to remain friends and help us when we needed it, but they were afraid to do it in the public eye because of the stigma associated with the Japanese in Hood River Valley.

Every home with sons in the service had a service flag with stars on the flag corresponding to the number of sons serving in the war effort. We had such a flag that we hung proudly in the window of our front room. It probably had four stars on it—for Tot, Min, Half, and Gene. My youngest brother Dick also volunteered for the army in January 1945 but served only a few months, until the war ended. One night a huge rock was thrown through that window. It woke my parents, and Ma wept as she picked up the rock from the parlor rug and retrieved the flag. On other occasions, people would steal gasoline out of our underground tanks. We had more ration stamps for gas because we were farmers, and people would come and steal the gas out of our pumps.

Then and many other times, Pa would call a family conference, even in the middle of the night, to help us face the current difficulties. It was like a scene in the dugout or in the team dressing room, with Pa as coach. Ma would say, "See? I told you things like this would happen. That's why I didn't want to come home." Pa would counter: "Just look at you. Sniffing and crying, just like they want us to. Yours is just the reaction they want. Give up and go away.

"All we are doing is living in our own home, minding our own business, a right which is just as much ours as it is theirs. We have a right to our homes and orchards. They can't scare or defeat us, and we mustn't let them. Besides, think of all the Japanese people waiting in camps, watching us. They may be discouraged from coming home if we fail to stand up against the minority here who are trying to chase us away."

In the succeeding days, as cars roared through our driveway late at night, as thieves stole gas, as persons jimmied up our tractor and trucks, as anonymous hate calls came in the night, as tools went missing from our woodshed and barn, Pa's periodic pep talks worked to recharge our batteries, enabling us to go out and play another inning. That took us through the worst years. At the same time, my father never made angry words or criticized anyone. He was very Zen: If he didn't like something, he was totally silent.

Sometimes people ask me whether my father ever considered leaving the United States. A few who came from Japan were planning to make money and go back to help their families, and a lot of Americans believed that was what they were all going to do, but my father never intended to return to Japan. There was no question he had come to this country to stay. I would say the same was true of at least 50 percent or more. They came to make their life here and intended never to return to Japan.

On a trip I made to Japan with my son Toby in the twenty-first century, we found letters my father wrote to his relatives, saying, "You know, I've worked hard here, and life has been very good. You might consider coming to the United States." That's the first time I heard or read anything like that from my father. He wrote that in 1952.

While we were struggling in Hood River, the War Relocation Authority, headed by Milton Eisenhower (brother to Dwight), was trying to close the camps. Many of the Japanese American citizens weren't leaving, however, because they didn't have a place to go, the way we did. We owned our property free and clear, so we were in the best possible situation. But so many other people had leased land for vegetable farming, and nobody would lease to them anymore. They had no other skills or occupation. For three years they had had no income, so what were they going to do?

They sat in the camps, and government officials worked on ways to get these people out so they could close the camps. The Department of Interior, which oversaw the War Relocation Authority, sent out photographers to take some beautiful pictures of my family on the farm. My brother Gene and my father were shown with apples on the trees. There were shots of my mother and sister with hoes, and my father pouring water into the tractor—all with smiles. According to the archive at the University of California, Berkeley, these photos were taken by Hikaru Iwasaki on May 21, 1945, just a month after we stepped off the train from camp and saw my brothers' names restored to the honor roll. Iwasaki was a Nisei who had also been imprisoned at Heart Mountain.[37]

At the time, no commercial mechanic would openly do repairs for us, stores were closed to us, nobody would walk to school with me. We didn't know what these pictures were taken for, but our friends in the camps told us later our images were put on display. We served as propaganda: *See these people? They are happily resettled in Hood River.* We looked happy even as we were being discriminated against.

Gene and Pa in a posed photograph for the WRA (Hikaru Iwasaki, War Relocation Authority, May 21, 1945)

Mika posed for the WRA (Hikaru Iwasaki, War Relocation Authority, May 21, 1945)

Not all Japanese American families returned to Hood River after the war. The Norimatsus had something like ten kids, and their orchard had not prospered before the war. The children ate dandelion greens and rice to survive. My father lent them money to buy sacks of rice. It was a small amount of money, but Mr. Norimatsu could not afford to pay it back for years and years.

A rare picture of Ma smiling, for the WRA (Hikaru Iwasaki, War Relocation Authority, May 21, 1945)

Like the sugar beet farmers who needed workers in Utah and who accepted Min out of the camps early, the Birds Eye factory in New Jersey, which processed frozen vegetables, needed able bodies. So most of the Norimatsu family went east.

Mr. Norimatsu finally paid back the borrowed sum, which my dad didn't need, but Pa always had great respect for this man because he honored the debt and never tried to write it off. By the time he paid it, the value of the goods would have been ten times that, maybe, but my dad always admired Mr. Norimatsu for making good on his debt. Clara Norimatsu was one of the daughters who married an employee of Birds Eye. My own family visited them in the summer of 1969 when we were on our way to Europe. One of the sisters remained in the Idaho region near the Minidoka camp, I believe.

Masuo Yasui, who used to give me candy in his store and whose son lost the legal fight against the curfew that went all the way to the Supreme Court, had been arrested by FBI agents only days after Pearl Harbor. Mr. Yasui spent the war in prison camps in Montana, Oklahoma, Louisiana, and finally New Mexico, isolated from his family, as a suspected spy and was not released until January 2, 1946. In a letter to my father two weeks later, sent from Denver, where he stayed briefly with two of his grown children, Mr. Yasui wrote:

> I spent a total of 1,488 long days, locked up. . . . The outpouring of kindness and consideration that I have received from you and some other friends, since the time of my incarceration to this day, is beyond description. I have no words to express my deep felt appreciation. I have been told by family members many times that when they submitted a petition to the authorities last year, they asked you to submit a useful and valuable document, and that it was of great help. You made it work. I would like to express my deepest gratitude to you for your friendship, which has never wavered. I hope I can return the favor to you someday. . . . I hope to return home as soon as possible to meet with you and have a friendly talk about our accumulated stories and future plans.[38]

But he could not go home. Though he stayed briefly with his son Chop on a Hood River farm, Mr. Yasui had lost his home, his store, and much of his farmland. Worst of all, he had lost his reputation. As Lauren Kessler wrote, though he had been known before the war as "the emperor" of the Hood River Nikkei community, Mr. Yasui was now a broken man whose "erstwhile friends were still whispering that he was a Japanese agent, a spy, a top-ranking officer in the Imperial Navy."[39] He and his wife Shidzuyo settled in southeast Portland to live on their savings and investments. Though he had maintained a stiff upper lip throughout his imprisonment, and proudly coached his wife to obtain US citizenship along with him in 1953, his mind began to wander, and on May 11, 1957, he committed suicide.[40]

Some of the story of these early postwar years in Hood River was related in newspapers and magazines of the time. Richard L. Neuberger, a staff writer for the Portland *Oregonian*, wrote a full-page article titled "All Quiet on Hood River as Japs Return to Valley," about the problems encountered by Japanese immigrants and their citizen-children when they returned to settle. It was published on June 16, 1946. The feature opened by quoting my brother, "Taro Asai . . . who was a staff sergeant with the 37th United States infantry division," and also quoted or mentioned many of the people I have described in this chapter: Carl Smith, the Reverend Sherman Burgoyne, Mrs. Max Moore, Fred Taylor (who was treasurer of Asbury Methodist), Sue Ogawa (and her daughters Lois and Kiyo, who were pictured at their water pump), and the League of Liberty and Justice. The feature also included a photo of Ma and Pa with our piano and portraits on it of their four oldest sons—several in uniform.[41]

Richard Neuberger's feature story in the June 16, 1946 Oregonian

Neuberger's article related the story of the honor roll incident and noted that "The Methodist minister [Burgoyne] said he had received letters from service men all over the world commending his stand in defense of the Hood River Japanese." Several of the racist residents were quoted, including Ralph Sherrieb and C. A. Perkins, as well as a rancher named J. F. Carnes, who claimed, "95 per cent of the folks in the county don't want the Japs back." There was a photo of the "Please Notice—No Jap Trade" sign in the window of Sherrieb's store at Rockford crossroads (opposite Mr. Steele's Rockford Store, which had a similar sign). But, Neuberger wrote, "the fact remains that the Japanese families are being assimilated back into the normal, everyday life of Oregon's busy fruit-raising mountain valley."

In the August 10, 1946, issue of the *Saturday Review of Literature*, Neuberger published "Their Brothers' Keepers,"[42] which was later condensed and reprinted in the *Reader's Digest*. It told much the same story as his *Oregonian* piece, but in a more lyrical, narrative, even passionate style, with lengthier quotes from Lois and Sue Ogawa, the Reverend Burgoyne, and my brother Tot. (Neuberger later served in the Oregon state legislature and the US Senate; a structure built on the Portland State University campus in the 1960s was named after him but underwent a $70 million remodel in 2018-19 and is now known as Fariborz Maseeh Hall.[43] The university transferred the Neuberger name to a different building on Southwest Fourth Avenue.)[44]

My brother Half served more than five and a half years in the army, during which time he went to the South Pacific, Australia, and the Philippines. He came home unexpectedly on Christmas Day 1945, unscratched and unharmed, from the Pacific theater. It was his last furlough before his discharge from the army.

Ma had a clock of her own in her mind, which accurately told her in the dead of the night what time it was, who came and went from the house, and all the details of such comings and goings.

That Christmas Eve was a complete puzzle to her, for she rose in the morning and said to us, "Two people went out last night; one came home at eleven o'clock and the other came home at about eleven-thirty; after midnight, another person came into the house and went upstairs." She could not bear the mystery any longer; she went upstairs to look and found Half asleep in his old room. The last we had known of his whereabouts, he was supposed to have been in the Philippines or Australia. After his discharge, Half went to Oregon State College on the G.I. Bill of Rights to study pharmacy.

About the same time, my brother Tot returned from the Pacific theater in uniform but was not yet discharged. He went into a store in town that did not do business with any of us. Although he was still wearing his uniform, the clerk refused him service. "I'm sorry, I can't sell to you," she told him. I don't know whether there was a "No Jap Trade" sign in the window of that store, but Tot knew why she had refused him service even though he was a US Army sergeant. She was just a young girl who was following instructions. She felt bad about the incident and tried to apologize. My brother turned and said, "Oh, that's all right. But actually I'm Chinese!"

This story was never known to us until my brother died some fifty years later. At his memorial service, the local minister said he had heard my brother tell the story on many occasions while visiting Tot over the years. The whole gathering burst out in laughter at his funeral. It struck me that my brother's reaction to this situation was just the kind of thing my father would say or do. He would bring light or humor to the tensest situations because he did not want to harbor negative emotions in himself or in other people. He had a way of doing that nonverbally, teaching us through his example.

My second brother, Min, was then dating Bessie Watanabe. She had gone to secretarial school with my sister Mika in Salt Lake

City and gotten a good job as a secretary in downtown Hood River. Her parents decided they were going to arrange a nice marriage for her to a rich farmer. Bessie was a sweet, obedient type of daughter. She went along with everything her family expected her to do—she even got engaged to the other man and went to Portland to pick out a ring—but she was still seeing Min on a regular basis. She'd drive to town from her house, and in between, she'd either come by our place or meet Min downtown.

At one point, her father came over and said, "I want your son to not see my daughter anymore." And my father said, "They're adults." (Min was 30, and Bessie was 24.) Mr. Watanabe turned verbally abusive, so my father told him, "Get out of my house."

As it got closer to the wedding with the other man, Bessie couldn't go through with it. So she and Min eloped. They went to Spokane, Washington, to be married by the minister who had been so supportive of our community through the war, the Reverend Sherman Burgoyne. We didn't know they were gone, and her parents didn't know. When they returned home after their marriage on February 17, 1948, it estranged Bessie from her parents. She did not return home, and neither of her parents ever came to visit Min and Bessie until their fourth child was born. They had Sam, Ellen, and Carl; and when Winston was about to be born, people kept coming to visit and asking, "Mr. Asai, why don't you forgive Mr. Watanabe's behavior, and fix that relationship?"

My father was a proud man, and he felt he had been insulted—and treated badly—by the other party. "He's not welcome in my house," Pa said. But my father liked Bessie very much, and he knew she was a sweet, gentle person. He said, "I feel really sorry for Bessie that she can't have this relationship with her mother," and so he relented. The past was kind of glossed over. The Watanabes came frequently to visit my parents after that, always bringing huge gifts. When I graduated from college, they gave me a nice present. But they never said, "I apologize for my bad behavior."

It's not as if they harmed us or anything, but in my father's view, it was the other person's obligation to say I'm sorry for the things I said or did. And Mr. Watanabe never did that.

In 1947, the Reverend Burgoyne was informed he was to be given the Thomas Jefferson Humanitarian Award from the Council against Intolerance in America, in a presentation at the Waldorf-Astoria Hotel in New York to be hosted by Eleanor Roosevelt. But he couldn't afford to travel to the East Coast to receive it. The grateful Japanese people of Hood River raised the money to pay for his train tickets to New York, hotel reservations, luggage, and expenses, so he could make the trip and receive the award. Other Japanese American Citizens League chapters, such as the one in Chicago, also held receptions for him along the way.[45]

But the Methodist Church split over the Reverend Burgoyne's friendship with and assistance to the Japanese Americans in Hood River. In June 1947, after he returned home, he was removed from his Hood River ministry and sent to a tiny church in Shedd, Oregon, which was no more than a wide place in the road south of Albany. Since the entire community of Shedd numbered 150 residents and the church membership totaled 89, it was a professional slap in the face.

Two Methodist district superintendents in Washington state intervened, and on July 27, 1947, Burgoyne was transferred again to the Hays Park church in Spokane.[46] He served the Spokane community for only eleven months (which was when he officiated for Min and Bessie's wedding) before returning to Oregon and ministering to various Methodist congregations in the Portland area through the 1950s, including Lents Methodist Church, Centenary-Wilbur Methodist Church[47] (where he officiated for Tot's wedding to Marie Namba on July 20, 1950),[48] and Sunnyside Methodist Church (where he oversaw the marriage of George Akiyama and Ruth Tomita on February 27, 1954; my brother Tot was an usher).[49]

On June 2, 1948, President Truman signed the Japanese American Evacuation Claims Act. It provided up to $25 million to compensate Japanese Americans for actual losses during their "evacuation." A pioneering piece of civil rights legislation, it unfortunately allowed the government to avoid any official admission of wrongdoing or its violation of our civil rights, and refused to compensate lost wages or anticipated profits, personal injury, pain and suffering, or any other costs related to the removal and incarceration. The Justice Department also stoutly contested every claim.[50]

The rumor went that if you thought you'd lost $40,000, you applied for $20,000, and if you were lucky, you'd get $10,000. That's roughly what happened. We had lost our original property, the one up in the hills that my father had created with his hands. He built the road, cut the timber, and planted the fruit trees. But because nobody would lease a property out in the boondocks, and you can't let an orchard go for three years, it withered. He had held on to it for sentimental reasons, but he finally sold it as pastureland for a big loss. Pa didn't want to apply for funds because it brought back too many painful memories; he had delivered six babies there.

My brother Min, who was about to be married, was going to buy an orchard of his own, a ranch for sale that he was planning to split with a buddy of his. He asked my dad if he would help him with the mortgage. "Why don't you apply for this evacuation claim," Min asked, "because it's been appropriated by Congress?" My dad said, "I don't really want to." Min offered to do the paperwork required to make a claim.

My brother just ahead of me, Dick, was pursuing his PhD in Champaign-Urbana, Illinois. My dad told Min to apply, and whatever financial support he could get, he could keep half for the mortgage on the property, and the other half would be sent to

Dick to finish his doctorate. So that's what happened. As I recall, Min lived on that new property as a single person for just a short while.

Min and Gene in US Army uniform in 1945. My fifth brother, Dick, also served briefly at war's end. (Asai family collection)

The Years of Social Isolation

I was in the seventh grade when our family returned to Hood River in April 1945, the first Japanese American student to reenter an elementary school in Hood River. Barrett Elementary School went through the eighth grade and was located just over a mile from our home. My childhood playmate Margaret Takagi's family was one that didn't come back; when I saw her in 1952, she was living in Ann Arbor, Michigan. Her friend Mary Sumoge returned to Hood River, but she went to Oak Grove School, about three miles up the road from our orchard in the opposite direction. So I was the only Japanese American girl in my elementary school through the entire seventh and eighth grades.

I was totally isolated and miserable as a 13-year-old. Each day I walked the distance to and from school alone. How painful it was for me to have no one to play with before and after school or during recesses and lunch hour. How much more painful it was to walk home alone, that long mile and a quarter, day after day for nearly a year from April 1945 to April 1946.

I needed to be around people even if they didn't speak to me, so I attended church every Sunday morning and went to the youth fellowship meetings every Sunday evening. This was a Christian church, the Disciples of Christ Church. The church was a little past the school, which meant it was more than a mile and a quarter from home, perhaps a mile and a half. I noted that if I sat in a pew where people were already sitting, they moved; and if I sat in an empty pew, no one else would sit there. I made it a point thereafter to sit in one of the smallest pews to the left of the aisle and nearest the wall (a sort of back of the bus on the side). I must admit to harboring mean thoughts, expressed in the temptation to sit in the longest pew so as to deprive worshippers of that many more seats.

In Sunday school, the only one to interact with me was Mr. Elmer Van Blaricom, who also taught shop at Hood River High School, although my classmates and peers sat around me. After the Sunday service, the congregation filed out of the church and shook the pastor's hand. I did the same, except that the pastor turned his head away from me as he shook my hand. He would never look me straight in the face, smile, or say anything to me directly. Later, he was replaced by Rev. Lawrence Porter, who with his wife made life much more pleasant for me.

I was baptized in that church when I was 14 or so. As time went on, some adult members of the church who saw me walking would pick me up and give me a ride, and eventually offered me a ride to church from my home. I remember especially Mrs. Veva Stranahan and Mrs. Klee, the daughter of Roy and Mary Hays, the people who had brought us the Christmas tree for our first holiday of the war in Tule Lake.

Mrs. Yeck was the principal of Barrett School and taught seventh and eighth grade at the same time. She was always friendly and helpful, and she felt sorry for me. During those years when I had no friends, she knew it would be painful for me to go out on the playground for recess, so she would ask me to clean the erasers and water the plants and such. She'd keep me in her room, doing those things, just to relieve the pain of isolation I was suffering.

Being with people was important to me, even if they treated me as though I were an invisible object. I had many hours, days, weeks, and months of meditation to contemplate the meaning of my life, my experiences, and my actions. I had thoughts of suicide, but I was too scared to do it. I don't remember thinking about poisoning, or anything else. But I did put a butcher knife under my pillow once; that was as close as I got.

While I lived alone in social isolation, my brother Dick was fortunate enough to have two close buddies in high school to pal around with. He and Dale Smith and Ralph Bisbee were like the Three Musketeers: going everywhere together and doing things together, in and out of school. It was their habit to go during the noon hour to a place referred to as "The Heights," a few blocks from school. There they would take turns buying three pints of ice cream to top off their lunches.

Now, if I saw a "No Jap Trade" sign in the window of any store, I avoided the place. Not Dick. He delighted in "trying them out." On one particular afternoon, it was Dick's turn to buy. The three boys went to a supermarket, where they picked out three pints of ice cream that Dick took to the counter to pay. Above the counter hung the sign.

The young clerk said, "I'm sorry, but I can't sell to you." Dick asked to know the reason. "Don't you see the sign?" Dick replied, "Well, I'm nearsighted. Why don't you put the sign out in the front, where I can see it?" Then he walked out of the store. His friend Dale Smith hurried into the store.

"Don't put that ice cream away. I'll take it," he said.

"Are you going to buy it for the fellow who was just in here?"

"And what if I am?"

"Because if you are, I can't sell it to you."

"Well, then, have your old ice cream!" Dale said with disgust, and he threw the ice cream onto the floor and walked out. My brother came home that night and told us the whole story, laughing uproariously as he did so. I listened, knowing that I would have wept in the store, had it been me.

Finally, just as I entered my adolescent years, a girl two years younger, Mae Vernon, broke my yearlong loneliness. The day that she chose to walk home with me was a day of sunshine in all ways, but my joy was soon marred. When we reached the West Side Store a quarter mile from school, Mae said, "Let's go in and buy some jawbreakers." I was flabbergasted that Mae had not noticed that for a year or more, the store had had a sign hanging on the glass door that read, "No Jap Trade."

I said nothing about it and made some excuse, perhaps that I didn't have any money and would rather just walk on ahead. Mae went in, bought some jawbreakers, ran to catch up with me, and shared her two-for-a-penny candy with me. Then, as we walked together up Markham Lane with swollen cheeks, one jawbreaker on each side, we met the misfortune of all misfortunes. Mrs. Bettsworth was coming down the road toward us.

Mrs. Bettsworth lived halfway between my house and the store. I had sweet memories in the prewar years of her inviting me to play in her tire swing after school each day. Mrs. Bettsworth's children were grown and gone, and she was lonely. I sang songs to her and told her stories in exchange for a cookie or a glass of milk.

Now this same woman yelled at me and threatened me with her dog. For almost a year I had had to pass by her house, morning and evening on my way to and from school, bearing insults and verbal abuse that she hurled at me. "Go back where you came from, you dirty Jap!" (And where was that?) or "Go home, dirty yellow Jap!" were the usual greetings. Worst of all, she would sic her dog on me.

It was bewildering and terrifying. Her house sat back from the road, which had a deep ditch alongside it. Tall weeds grew between the house and the ditch. I tried everything to avoid confronting her on my daily walks to and from school. I tried to sneak quietly by and walk in the ditch behind the tall weeds so as not to be seen, but nothing worked. I am sure she watched the clock and waited for me, for she was always there to yell at me as I went by.

Knowing of the training and obedience of her dogs from pre-war days made me doubly fearful of her dog. I was sure it would bite me, and I was determined to win the battle against the dog through sheer superiority of will and mind. I reasoned that if the dog knew I was scared, he would bite me. If my face showed fear, he would know I was scared, because the truth is that I *was* scared. If I ran, he would know, too, that I was afraid. Therefore I vowed to outsmart him by not showing him my face and somehow fooling him into thinking that I was not at all afraid.

To accomplish this, I decided to always turn my head away from the dog when it came running toward me—snarling, growling, curling its lip, and showing its teeth. In addition, I devised ways of walking to prevent myself from running. I did this through 100 percent effort of will and mind, putting one foot ahead of the other, touching heel to toe, heel to toe.

The dog never bit me, but when its cold, wet nose touched my leg (which happened more than once), it was like an electric shock, almost worse than being bitten. Tears rolled down my cheeks, either from fear of being bitten or from relief at not being bitten, I don't know which. Sometimes I actually wished that the dog would bite me and get it over with. The agony of anticipation of being bitten was nearly as bad as an actual bite.

As Mae and I walked up the road and got closer to Mrs. Bettsworth, I walked faster and faster ahead of Mae. I was not anxious to be around for the confrontation. Mae asked, "Why are you going so fast?" and I waved at her. When I thought Mrs. Bettsworth was up to where Mae was, I turned around to see what was going to happen. I saw Mrs. Bettsworth put her hands on her hips and say, "Why, Mae Vernon, I thought that you had more respect than to walk with a dirty, yellow Jap!"

Mae was a nervous, high-strung little girl. She opened her

mouth to make a reply, but nothing came out. Her face merely turned red hot with anger, and she began to shake all over. Finally, she yelled at me to come back. "Come to my house. We'll tell my parents, and they'll fix Mrs. Bettsworth." I thought: *Oh, sure. Your mother's a teacher at my school and she's never spoken to me; your father is a mechanic who won't work on our tractors, cars, and trucks. That's the end of Mae Vernon walking with me, I guess.* I waved and went home.

Mae's family were good Mormons, and although they might not personally help us, as a matter of principle, the group could act in our behalf. They stood up for what was right when it was not too public and if it was on an individual basis, where nobody else was around. Lots of people were like that in those postwar years. People would help us in invisible ways, but they wouldn't dare to say hello to us in town, on the street, or in church. That's what happens when people don't have a backbone.

Mae's family had been buying butter, eggs, milk, and more from Mrs. Bettsworth. They stopped doing so and told Mrs. Bettsworth that the reason was her treatment of Mae and me. The Vernons then went to Mrs. Bettsworth's church (which was my church, too), where she attended the Thursday Ladies' Aid Society, to report this incident. Subsequently, a group of persons from the church—some of whom, no doubt, had never spoken to me at services—paid Mrs. Bettsworth a visit and reprimanded her for her behavior.

After the church visitation, Mrs. Bettsworth no longer yelled at me or sent her dog after me, but she walked to the road with the dog. With her arms crossed, she watched me silently as I walked by each day, as if to say, "All right, you've won. I can't yell at you or send my dog after you, but that doesn't stop me from coming out to the road to glare at you as you go by." I didn't care at all, however, for the thought of the dog being held back was enough to make my days beautiful.

Not long after the Mae Vernon incident, the church had a benefit spaghetti dinner, with the youth of the church serving as waiters and waitresses. After everyone was served, it was our turn to eat. As I stood in line to get some spaghetti, Mrs. Bettsworth, who was serving it up at the time, looked up and saw me. She dropped the spoon and walked away. Another lady hastily stepped up and served my plate in silence. I think only three people were aware of the incident.

I had not confided in my family about the trouble I had been having to and from school or the social isolation I had been experiencing at school and church. The incident with Mrs. Bettsworth in front of Mae Vernon was broadcast about somewhat, though. My eldest brother learned of it through a friendly neighbor, Arne Hukari. (He had a Finnish background, as did many people in Hood River. His mother lived with him and his family for years. She spoke only Finnish, and I remember hearing her chatter in that language on our party line.)

My brother questioned me about the incident with Mrs. Bettsworth, but I passed it off as just a small matter. It was now a thing of the past, after all. Although I'm sure my parents and my brother worried about me, I was glad there was no further discussion about it. I knew they were weighted down with matters of greater import in our struggle to return and reaffirm our right to live in our home community, and it was an embarrassment to me to add to their burden.

About thirty years later, I made a special effort to locate Mae. She was living in Salem, Oregon, with her husband and family. They had moved because they had a deaf child who was attending the Oregon School for the Deaf there. I asked if she remembered the first day she walked home with me. She replied, "How could I forget?"

Years later, Mae's daughter telephoned me to inform me of her mother's death. It was perhaps 2006. We had never met, but Mae had spoken about me to her daughter often. She felt that she knew me and that I would want to know about her mother's passing.

There was another girl who was kind of friendly from afar, partly because she was two grades below me and lived a mile in the other direction from school. Her name was Jeanette Sargeant. I have a feeling she would have walked home with me if she had lived on the same road to my house. I also saw her at Sunday school because she and her two brothers went to the same church.

I graduated from the eighth grade at Barrett School in June 1946. The following September, I caught the bus into town to Hood River Junior High School (grades seven, eight, and nine for the "town kids," but only grade nine for us "country kids" who attended elementary school through the eighth grade).

On the first day of school, several of us missed the bus home. Most of the students called their families to be picked up, but Cherie Frey and I had to find our own way home. I lived on a farm (apple orchard), and would never consider calling my family to come after me; they probably wouldn't have answered the phone anyway, since Ma worked in the orchard all day, too. Cherie's parents were the type that would not pick her up even if she were to call them. I recall that she seldom participated in after-school or evening activities because of the distance she lived from school (about eight miles) and the transportation problems.

There we were, the two of us. We started walking together out of town. As we left The Heights, we approached the home of her grandparents. Cherie's parents were divorced, her mother had remarried, and Cherie was living with her mother and stepfather. These grandparents were her father's parents, with whom she had limited relations, much like with her father. These grandparents, then, had little contact with her mother. It was an awkward situation, to say the least.

Cherie said, "I know! My grandparents live right here. I'll ask my grandfather to take us home." I froze, realizing that Cherie's grandfather must be George Frey, the new leader of the anti-Japanese movement for American Legion Post No. 22. I let Cherie go into her grandparents' house alone and walked on ahead myself. In a little while, a car stopped to pick me up. Cherie had of course urged her grandfather to stop to "pick up a friend."

Her grandfather never spoke, never looked left or right, nor at me. He just looked straight ahead and took us home. His wife sat beside him in the front seat and spoke to me in a friendly way. Cherie chattered all the way while I sat in the back seat with her, paralyzed with fear, until they let me off at the corner to my house. Never was I so relieved to get out of a car. I think I would have preferred to walk the whole five miles home to suffering through the discomfort of that ride.

I had been given a Japanese name, as had all my brothers and sisters. My name was Mitsuko, pronounced "mee-tsu-co," and I'd been Mitsuko all my life. But my friends and all my classmates called me "MITTS-uh-ko" or "mit-SOO-ko." After suffering discrimination, walking walk to and from school alone, having no one to play with at recess, and sitting alone in a pew at church, I thought that it was no fun to be Japanese. Now I was riding a bus to school in town, and I thought, *Town kids don't know I'm Mitsuko, so I think I'll become 0 percent Japanese and 200 percent American. I'm gonna be Mitzi.*

So I went to junior high school and registered as Mitzi. I didn't tell anybody, not even my father. My first report card came home, and my dad looked at it and saw "Mitzi Asai." And he looked at me and smiled. As a Zen Buddhist, he didn't say anything or ask questions. The subject never came up. I have been Mitzi ever since. I didn't even have to go to court to change my name.

After a year and a half alone in the seventh and eighth grades, I was included in church and social activities during my high school years. In the matter of boy-girl relations, however, there was a fine line between what was acceptable and what was possible. I suffered during that time because of course I wanted to date, and I wanted to go dancing. But I never even learned how to dance. It wasn't until I was a high school teacher in the mid-1950s that my students taught me how to dance while I chaperoned their dances. In 2017, I went to the sixty-first high school class reunion of my Creswell students, just as I had attended so many previous reunions, and the man who taught me how to dance in the 1950s said to me, "let's dance."

Summer church camp in the late 1940s (Asai family collection)

At the end of ninth grade, the big event of the year was a dance at the Columbia Gorge Hotel, the ninth-grade formal. It was a big event, like a junior or senior prom for upper-class high schoolers. I can't remember if we even had to pay anything—it might have been financed by the school. One of the teachers, Mrs. Beard, who I think felt sorry for me, asked if I planned to attend the dance. I said I didn't think so, because secretly I feared that no one would dance with me. She encouraged me to go even if I didn't have a date. The dance was going to include a nice banquet and presented the opportunity to dress up.

So I was talked into going. One of the chaperones was the step-father of one of the girls who was going to be a high-school class-mate. He was a White Russian who had escaped Russia and mar-ried an American woman, and he was the only one who danced with me. He danced with me several times because he could see I didn't have any partners. He was probably in his forties or fifties, and at the time he seemed to me to be so old. But I was so happy just to be able to dance (even if not very well), to put on a long dress, and to be among my peers, who were friendly to me by that time, though not dating material.

Eventually I became president of the church youth group, even if they weren't associating with me much. I don't remember whether I was elected or appointed. It was kind of encouraged by the rever-end's wife, Mrs. Porter, because I seemed to be a leader type. That's when Mrs. Steele said in her gossip column, "Mitzi Loftus is now president of the youth group at Valley Christian Church."

By the time I graduated in 1950, I had been president of the church youth group and gone to summer camp with the others, so it was all right for me to go out "with the gang" or to grab a Coke with a boy, as long as it was not just me and a boy but instead part of a larger group. Attendance at any sports events, dances, or other school activities had to be as a single, or "stag." After church activities, Jeanette, Jim, and Rollo Sargeant; my classmate

Mary Moore and her boyfriend Earl Richards; and Mary's cousin Barbara Moore might be there. Mary's older sister was friendly, too, although she was not in our social circle.

Toward the end of high school, there were two Japanese American boys in my class, and it was expected that if I were to have a date, I should go out with one of them. But I had absolutely no interest in either of these boys. I love to go to high schools and talk about this now, because I know how to get to the listeners. I say, "How would you like it if they told you you could only date two boys in high school? Of course, one of them's stupid and the other one's ugly (I exaggerate a bit), but that's your choice." Even if I had been interested in them and had gone to a dance with them, I'd have had to dance with one or the other all night because nobody else would dance with me.

So I went without dating, until the night of my graduation from high school. That night I gave in to going out with one of those boys, but I cannot say that it brought me any great fun. In fact, the experience was a little painful, so I asked to be taken home early. My first real dates were in college.

When he was in the army, my brother Tot had arranged a subscription to *American Girl* magazine for me. It's a Girl Scout magazine, and I was in Camp Fire Girls, but my brother didn't know that. But that was fine; the magazine was fun, and it meant I got mail every month. The August 1949 issue had a story called "Girl without a Country?" It was an excerpt from the book *It Might Be You*, by Ruth Adams Knight, which was due to be published that fall.[1]

The story opens with Rosebud Yusuki and her family returning to their run-down "small truck farm" after spending the war in camp. It does not specify her age or the location—it sounds as if she might be in middle school in California—but lots of details were familiar. Early in the story, it says, "she hadn't minded the relocation camp as much as some of the other girls had. She had been small when it had begun." Rosebud's older brother Joe enlisted right after Pearl Harbor, had "infrequent furloughs" to visit the family in camp, and was reported missing in action in the Pacific, but returned home after having lost a leg.

"In class she was one of the good students. . . . But at recess and after school it wasn't the way it had been before at all," the story goes on. All her old friends—Selma, Marion, her former best friend Myrtle, and especially Sally—repeatedly shun Rosebud, and she is ejected from the club of girls who'd been together since first grade. They tell her 'You started a war,' which was a 'wicked, treacherous thing.' Sally insists 'You're a Jap.'" The story ends, "she looked at the angry faces about her and saw it wasn't any use. What they felt had nothing to do with facts. To people like them, she knew, a Japanese would be a Jap forever and forever."

When I read that article, I said, "That's my story. It's exactly the same thing I experienced." So I thought, I'm going to write a letter to the editor. It was printed in the November issue. I said, in part, "I was terribly disappointed with the end. Usually, a story ends happily. And yet, if it had turned out that way, it would not be true, as far as I can see." I said I had been sent to the camps, and when I came home, things weren't the same. "The first year or two of school was very lonesome and dreary." None of my friends would say to my face why they didn't want me around at certain times, "but I knew they wouldn't be served even if they let me go in."

"Now things are almost the same as they used to be," my letter continued, "and yet, there is that certain feeling, which I wonder how long will be with me. Everyone goes in couples, and I am the only extra," I said, "but they say they don't mind me along at all. Many boys are very nice to me and seem to like me, but they won't ask me out, so that's why I was so interested in what would happen to Rosebud and was very disappointed. Do not think all this makes me feel bitter, but I admit it makes me feel depressed at times. I try to go on with my chin up, and I manage to get along, but I often think about this."[2]

Ruth Adams Knight saw my letter and wrote to me. She said she was glad to see my letter to the editor and that what appeared in the magazine was only an excerpt from the book she had written. We corresponded for a while; she sent me a Christmas newsletter for several years after that. My letter also attracted an array of pen pals. For a time, I exchanged letters with a girl in Hawaii; a girl in Muscatine, Iowa; a girl in Greece; and one in England. My friend in Florida, Tommy Pierson, was a Girl Scout leader, and she made it possible for me to make a six-week trip to the eastern United States after my sophomore year of college, in 1952. She gave me a bus ticket to St. Louis, Missouri, and scribbled the name of her friend there on a piece of sheet music, "Meet Me in St. Louis." From there I went to Tennessee, where I met up with Tommy, who took me through Great Smoky Mountains National Park to Niagara Falls and New York City.

An American soldier stationed in Tokyo read the magazine in the post library and wrote that he was intrigued by my life story since he was originally from Elgin, Illinois, and was now in Japan with the Occupation. I actually tried to see him when I passed through Chicago on that 1950s trip, but I think I only talked to him on the telephone there because it didn't work out for us to meet.

I also saw Mr. Hachiya, Frank and Homer's father, in Chicago. He was so lonely. His wife was still alive in Japan then, and he kept saying, "I wish she had never gone home." Then he finally said, *Shikataganai*—that characteristic Japanese expression which means it can't be helped, you just have to live with it. And he said, "It seems stupid for me to die in the United States and for her to die in Japan, so I'm gonna go back to Japan." So he returned to the old country, and I saw him once more with his wife in Okayama, but he survived only a couple years and died of unhappiness, I think, because he told me he hated living in Japan.

By far the most important pen pal that came out of the *American Girl* story and my letter was Phyllis Grubb in Roanoke, Virginia, with whom I kept up a correspondence for almost seventy years. We went through high school—and I think she went to college for a couple years but did not complete it—our marriages, our children, and then we met for the first and only time at her home in Roanoke in 1969, when my husband and I and our three boys were on our way to New York to catch a freighter to Morocco and the two years we spent in Europe.

Her married name was Phyllis Grubb Harmon. She was the most fun human being, and totally a person of the world who loved people—it didn't matter who they were or what they were—though she had grown up in a typical Southern home. And she loved me from the start. When we were visiting her, she said, "Mitzi, I'm not going to introduce you to my parents, because they are racist. And if they said one unpleasant word to you, it would break my heart."

Her daughter Georgiana was only about 5 years old when she saw me, but she knew about me and sent me birthday cards sometimes. She preceded her mother in death by a few years, and when Phyllis sent me her daughter's death notice, it said, "she is survived by" (and there was a list of her mother, her aunts, and cousins) "and her dear friend, Mitzi Loftus of Oregon." It just made me cry. Phyllis died in December 2016. Over nearly seventy years of correspondence, I spent time in this wonderful woman's company for only two or three days.

CHAPTER 12

The 1950s

My brother Half was honorably discharged from the army in 1946 after serving five and a half years. In September 1949, he had been studying at Oregon State College on G.I. Bill benefits for three years and was preparing to begin his senior year. The pharmacy course in which he enrolled had not yet been extended to a five-year course. I was a junior in high school by then.

I remember Half talking to my dad about borrowing money to buy a drug store in Mexico after he finished school, or maybe Pa told me about this. Half had studied Spanish, and I guess he thought he would be more welcome there than in the United States, where there was still much prejudice. He asked my dad to lend him money, and our father said yes.

Years later, when I was attending the University of Oregon in Eugene, I would sometimes visit a close friend of Half's in Portland we knew as "Mother Mary." Mary Taniguchi, an Issei born in Japan in 1902, had lived in The Dalles with her daughters Helen and Mable. Half would visit them there because I think he was sweet on Mable. When we were at Pinedale Assembly Center in 1942, they lived close to us, and Mable, who would have been 16 when I was 10, treated me like a little sister. Of course, Half was not there, having left for the army the summer before.

Half with an Army buddy (Asai family collection)

After the Taniguchis returned from camp, they lived in Portland, where Mary operated a hotel. Because our mother didn't speak much English, Half rarely confided in her. Instead, he turned to "Mother Mary." He told her that he was going to ask me if I would be interested in studying pharmacy at Oregon State; and if I did, he would hire me at his store in Mexico. I only learned about this part of it later.

Half worked hard every day in the harvest season that fall of 1949, up to the day he took the family car and drove to Corvallis with all his college baggage as well as that of two other brothers, Gene and Dick, who were also attending Oregon State. Returning the car to Hood River late at night, exhausted from working and driving, he fell asleep on the road.

In a bend in the highway, the car rolled off the Columbia River Highway and down a steep embankment on the river side. There were railroad tracks down below, close to the water's edge. The car hit a tree on the way down, bounced off, and landed squarely on the tracks.

Half told Pa that he woke up when the car hit the tree. With difficulty, he pulled himself out of the car and scrambled up the rocky slope to the highway—a climb of about 150 feet. A few minutes later, Half watched as a train came by and knocked the car off the tracks. It was perhaps two or three o'clock in the morning, the darkness illuminated somewhat by moonlight.

The people who picked up Half and gave him a ride to Hood River Hospital had seen the whole sequence of events and stayed at the hospital long enough to relate the details to Pa and brother Tot. They had watched my brother's car weave on the road before he went over the cliff. They assumed he was drunk and therefore did not try to overtake him. He showed them his billfold and identification and asked them to take him to Hood River, about twenty miles away.

Their vehicle was a sort of makeshift pickup. With three persons already in it, Half was forced to ride out in the open air in back. When he arrived at the hospital, he asked for a bed immediately. Since he had no evident scars or wounds, they put him off. The hospital was overcrowded and busy with the victims of another accident. After sitting a while, Half got up and said angrily and in desperation, "If you don't find me a bed, I'll find one myself!" He walked toward the elevator but fainted before he reached it. Then the hospital attendants rushed to take care of him. There were no available rooms, so they partitioned off a bed in the hallway with curtains, and that is where he was seen the next day, after surgery.

The hospital called to report Half's accident. Pa and Tot hurried to the hospital. Pa arrived and saw the people sitting in the waiting room from the other accident, which made his heart beat fast. He assumed that they all had something to do with the accident Half had been involved in. When Pa learned that Half had been in a one-car accident, he felt a little relieved.

Pa and Tot were able to see Half, who was not fully coherent. He kept fussing about having lost his wallet and would talk of nothing else. Pa and Tot went home, knowing that Half would undergo exploratory surgery later that day. They went back to the hospital in time to see Half come out of surgery. The doctor told them that the young man would live and would be faced with several months of convalescence. They went home relieved and did not return to visit that evening, to give him needed rest after surgery. They themselves were in need of rest after the long night and a day of hard work on the harvest before and after the accident.

In the middle of the night, another call came from the hospital to inform us that Half had died. Pa was extremely angry, having been assured that his son would recover. He ordered an autopsy, which revealed that Half's internal organs had been displaced and damaged, and his pancreas destroyed. Pa and Tot were extremely sorry they had not stayed with Half, but they had believed what the doctor had told them. The truth of his condition had not been revealed. Ma had no opportunity to see her son at all.

The whole family felt helpless and betrayed. I had slept through both nights, but when Tot came into my room the morning after Half died without saying a word, I knew what his message was. The awful meaning of death reached me for the first time, at the age of 17. Pa's comment was, "He didn't even get to have a room in the hospital. He had to die in the hallway with only a wall of curtains around him." The date was September 25, 1949.

My oldest brother didn't marry until the next summer. Tot was 35 in 1950, and my father was kind of concerned. But he was half Americanized—liberal-minded for a Japanese man—and didn't believe in arranging a marriage for his children, which many of his peers still tried to do. *Baishakunin*, the go-betweens in Japanese culture, would come and arrange a marriage for your son. The more respected you were, the more people would come and try to help you find a wife for your son. My father figured his children would find their own spouses.

Many situations like that would come up. My dad would say, "Mr. Sato thinks that you might marry this girl." So Tot would say, "Okay, I'll date her." He'd take her out for a few dates and that would be it, because it wasn't somebody he wanted to marry.

Eventually, he found his own wife, Marie Namba, who had grown up in Fairview, a town east of Portland near the mouth of the Columbia Gorge, and who had graduated from Gresham High School just before the war. Her family had been imprisoned at the Minidoka camp in Hunt, Idaho. Tot married her on August 20, 1950.

I graduated from Hood River High School that summer. By this time, I had earned the respect of my peers, but boys still would not date me. I served as student body treasurer, sang three years in Glee Club, was active in Pep Club, served as usher at concerts and programs, and sold many a hot dog at football games. Out of a class of seventy-seven, I was the valedictorian and delivered the valedictory speech at the commencement exercises.

The faculty had selected me to apply for large, highly competitive scholarships statewide and regionally. I did not have the sense to apply for other, lesser scholarships that would have been more within my reach. No counselor or teacher advised me in these matters. As a result, I graduated without receiving promises of any financial aid. I moped through the summer and threw the only tantrum in my life when Pa said he intended to send me to business college. I told him I'd rather stay home and work on the farm the rest of my life than go to business college. His eyes widened, and he realized for the first time how serious I was about getting a university education. Others later remarked that Pa had correctly sensed my business abilities but had not taken into account my interest level.

Our neighbor, Mrs. Moller, and a high school teacher, Mrs. Bolinger, heard about my predicament, and the two began to work on helping me. A Reed College graduate, Mrs. Bolinger hoped to interest me in her alma mater. Mrs. Moller was a graduate of the University of Oregon, and she tried to get financial aid for me there. It was already August, and Reed College had filled its admission quota. All the scholarships had likely been awarded.

Mrs. Moller had a friend, Karl Onthank, who was chairman of the scholarship committee at the University of Oregon. The university was able to offer me a hundred-dollar scholarship, one that had been turned down by its recipient. That, plus a live-in room-and-board job with the family of the newly hired dean of men, were the encouragement I needed to enter the University of Oregon in the fall of 1950. I used the scholarship award as a wedge to convince Pa that going to Eugene to study was a good idea. I told him the scholarship was an honor that I should not turn down. Pa's practical Asian response was, "How do you expect to go to college on $100?"

"I can work for my room and board. I also have saved $365 in the bank!"

"So you think you can go to school on $465, huh?"

"I'd like to try."

"And what about the other three years?"

"Well, I think something will work out, and if it doesn't, I'll work and save money until I could go back."

"Well, all right, then. Try it for a year and see how it goes."

I wrote a letter to the dean of women, asking for help. She was the one who "created" the room-and-board job for me by twisting the dean of men's arm, I later found out. I stayed with the Ray Hawk family: babysitting, housecleaning, helping with meals, washing, and doing anything else that needed to be done. Mr. Hawk called me the automatic dishwasher, but he acknowledged that I had more personality than the mechanical type. I became another member of the Hawk family for two years. Kenneth Alan was 5 years old, and Billy Lee was 3. Both would marry and have children of their own. Ken became a practicing dentist in Eugene.

Since the Hawks entertained many persons in the university community socially, I came to meet some of my professors personally and in an informal setting. Dr. Paul Kambly of the School of Education was a close friend of the Hawks, as was Bill Bowerman, who later became known as the father of jogging, coach to Olympic runner Steve Prefontaine, and one of the founders of the Nike Company.

After two years in the Hawk household, and with Mr. Hawk's help on the scholarship committee, I received some kind of scholarship in each of the first three years: Oregon Mothers', state fee, and $350 from Tri-Delta. The last two years of undergraduate study, I lived in Carson Hall, a relatively new dormitory where, as a senior, I was sponsored by the girls in the dorm. Traditionally, a foreign student received the sponsorship. Dean of Women Golda Wickham warned them that this had never been done and would set a precedent.

The action came about largely as a result of the efforts of Mrs. Stokes, the house mother, and the house council, of which I was a member. That was the only time the house council took a vote on a matter I didn't know what was being voted on, though I was present. This amounted to the dormitory girls' paying for my board bill for the year, in return for nothing except for me to remain in Carson Hall. I had planned to move out and into a cooperative house to reduce costs.

I was flattered to receive aid and interest from Mrs. Stokes, a dignified woman with a stern appearance. The girls in the dormitory sometimes made jokes, saying that Mrs. Stokes's face would crack if she were to smile. Not many girls were invited into her apartment for tea. When they were, they had to be on their best behavior and practice their finest manners.

I surmise that most of the girls who never saw the lighter side of Mrs. Stokes were the frequent violators of the house rules and regulations, the ones who felt the house mother's axe fall on their neck. Closing time at the dormitory was an unpleasant period for the house mother and the night custodians as they tried to separate the many couples locked in embraces on the front entry, making their heated, prolonged farewells. Securing the door for the night was not possible without this nightly ritual. I think Mrs. Stokes was referring to this situation when I once tried to serve her some carrots in the cafeteria line.

"No carrots, please," said Mrs. Stokes.

"But Mrs. Stokes. Carrots are good for your eyes. You can see better in the dark," I teased.

"I can see well enough in the dark, thank you!" was her retort.

In college, I lived in the dormitories. I could hardly believe it when my classmates would say, "Oh my god, my parents are coming for the weekend! I hope they don't stay more than two days." Or they'd be on the phone and say, "The food is terrible, Mom! If it weren't for the cookies you send me every month, I don't think I could stand it." Or "I just sent my dirty clothes to you." College students sending their dirty laundry home for their parents to wash? These kinds of conversations were just so startling and horrifying to me.

With the house sponsorship, for the first time I had spending money beyond the payment of needed college expenses. I continued working in the dormitory cafeteria, as I had done the previous year. Besides, some of my best friends were in the Carson kitchen crew. I took the whole kitchen crew to Tino's Spaghetti House for dinner in the spring quarter, just before I graduated, since I had spare funds. I also bought an engraved silver plate for Carson Hall, which I saw there more than thirty years later, in 1986. It was used at a reception when Michi Yasui Ando received her diploma forty-four years late, in the special ceremony at the commencement that June (described in chapter 7).

In the spring of 1954, I received a telephone call from Wayne Foster, the president of the Rotary Club in Hood River. He told me that the local chapter had selected me to apply for the Rotary Fellowship Study Abroad. I said, "Are you sure? This is *me*!" Although I had been the valedictorian of my high school graduating class and been invited to speak to this Rotary chapter four years before, the club was not noted for being openly friendly toward Japanese people in Hood River.

The man who called me was the new superintendent of schools, but he was also new in town and knew nothing of Hood River's previous history. As chairman of the selection committee, he must have examined my high school record and college records, then suggested my name as the fellowship candidate. Everyone else on the committee may have been too embarrassed to veto the nomination and be forced to give a reason for voting against my candidacy.

I filled out the application with the hope of studying French at the University of Grenoble. Dr. Harry Crooks, retired president of Albany College (later Lewis and Clark College) told me that I came in second to a young man at Linfield College. Dr. Crooks was one of the judges of this competition and had voted for me right up to the end, insisting that I should have received the fellowship. He revealed that there were two factors against me in the eyes of the Rotary committee: my sex and my ethnicity. Dr. Crooks said these factors biased the other members of the committee. Remnants of discrimination were evident nearly a decade after the end of the war, though by that time nobody had the nerve to call me a Jap to my face or refuse to sell me something in a store.

I had mentioned my experiences to my fellow kitchen crew in the dorm, and they said, "Well, there isn't that kind of discrimination here in Eugene, is there?" I said, well, maybe not in town, but in the outskirts there is. They said, "Oh, it's just your imagination, Mitzi." So I challenged them to a little experiment. With one of them as my date, we went up the McKenzie River to Albert's Lodge, an ideal place to have a dinner date before the junior or senior prom. It was about thirty miles east of Eugene at a tiny town called Vida. My date and I were not treated like the other patrons: we waited a long time to get waited on, were spoken to curtly, and

College graduation, the University of Oregon, 1954 (Loftus family collection)

we decided to leave without eating there. On our way home, my date said, "You're right."

In June 1954, I received my bachelor of arts. I was a member of Mortar Board, a senior women's honorary, and Phi Beta Kappa, a scholastic honorary.[1] The latter I was elected to by being "scraped from the bottom of the GPA barrel," as Dr. Lesch put it. Dr. Lesch was one of the best teachers I had at the university. He was unforgettable when he held his students spellbound in classes on epic literature and Milton.

I signed my first contract to teach at Creswell Union High School, twelve miles south of Eugene. A little later, after I'd married, one of my students said to me, "Mrs. Loftus! What kind of name is that? Where are you from?" I joked, "Well, just look at my face; can't you tell I'm Norwegian?" Oregon had a civil rights law that prohibited mention of one's race on any job application papers. One of my professors complained that a letter of recommendation he had written for me was returned because he mentioned I was of Japanese extraction. He had to rewrite the letter and delete that fact from the original.

This same mentor, Professor Pierce-Jones, offered me a graduate assistantship to work on a longitudinal study of child-rearing practices among certain Native American tribes. I was sorely tempted by this offer but opted to teach school immediately instead of doing graduate study and postponing teaching experience. The superintendent of schools in Creswell, Professor Edwin Ditto, who was also principal of the high school where I taught for the next three years, offered me a contract but asked after a personal interview if I would be willing to attend a school board meeting to meet the members of the board before signing it. He wanted them all to see what he was getting them into. I appreciated his thinking and agreed to do it. The board gave me a warm reception and were supportive of me for the two years I taught at their high school.

In 1980 and 1981, I attended the twenty-fifth class reunion of my students, who had been seniors in the first years of my teaching career. I was presented with a watercolor picture done by one of my students. In 1985 and 1986, I attended the thirtieth class reunions of these students, by which time I received another picture done by the same artist. Both hang on the walls of my home. Some of these same students went on a cruise to Alaska in 2012 to help me celebrate my 80th birthday. They were all 74 years old by that time.

Ma and Pa in 1954, the year I graduated from college (Loftus family collection)

CHAPTER 13

Masako

Remember my oldest sister, Masako, who had been left with in-laws in Japan at the behest of my father's mother back in 1916? What happened to her and her family from the years just before World War II to the present seems like a fairy tale.

When Masako reached marriageable age, her uncle and future in-laws arranged for her to marry. Her husband was the only son of a wealthy family in Nagoya, Japan's third largest city. Shortly after their marriage, her husband was sent to Manchuria in the Sino-Japanese War. Japanese soldiers in that conflict would rarely return home alive. This man's parents—her in-laws, who had had a hand in arranging the marriage—began to worry about the possibility of his death and the loss of their inheritance.

Unbeknownst to Masako, they planned a divorce for her, which was legal and common in that day and age. They sent her back "home," to the uncle's place where she had grown up. By this time, however, she was already pregnant. In Japan, it is common for a woman to return to her mother's home to give birth to her first child, so Masako naturally assumed this was the reason for her return to the country, away from her in-laws in the city.

When her child was born several months later, she dutifully reported the birth of a son to the paternal grandparents. But this news merely served to worry them further, for the baby would be a male heir—something they did not wish to acknowledge. One day they arrived at her uncle's house, where Masako and the baby were staying, and asked to see her uncle. He was working in the rice paddies, which were located a good distance away from the house, and only Masako and her baby were home.

Masako went to call her uncle in, and while she was gone, her in-laws took the baby and fled. They put the infant up

My oldest sister Masako in Japan, probably about 1935 or 1936 (Asai family collection)

for adoption, and he was taken in by a childless couple on the west coast of the main island of Honshu. The foster father was an employee of the national railway. In conversations I had with relatives about this twenty years later, I was told that Masako was heartbroken; in their words, "Her spirit died with the loss of her baby."

She left her uncle's house, where she felt she had already been a burden and to which she now believed she had brought shame on account of her troubles. She returned to Nagoya, where she had lived in the interim with her in-laws. Her husband from the arranged marriage was indeed killed in the Sino-Japanese war, never to see his family again or to learn that his wife had borne him a son.

Masako subsequently remarried, and her second husband did not enter the armed services, perhaps due to poor health. During the World War II years, civilians in Japan were "drafted" to do reconstruction work in other parts of the country. It was during one of these projects that he was away from Nagoya, when the American B-52s flew over and set the city on fire. Since it contained a major airplane factory, Nagoya became a prime bombing target.

Masako was still in the city with what we believe to be two children by the second marriage. This was odd, because nearly everyone in the city had fled to the hills for safety. Her house caught fire in the bombings. A child from the neighbor's house told the following story (which was given to us second- or thirdhand): "Masako was visiting my house when her house started on fire. Looking out the window and seeing her house on fire, she cried, 'My babies, my babies!' and ran out and into her own house, never to be seen again."

All of Nagoya suffered severe losses, and it took many days to assess the damage and locate survivors. No signs of either my sister or her children were ever found. We have to assume she suffocated or burned to death with her children. Her husband was likely to have survived her, but he made no subsequent attempt to contact any of the relatives, and no one was ever able to locate him.

We learned almost a year later that US bombers began to target Nagoya on April 18, 1945. We returned home to Hood River from our three years in the camps on April 20.

Thus my nephew, the kidnapped child of my oldest sister's first marriage, remained the sole survivor of Masako's branch of my family. Nothing was known about him until 1949, when he was about 11 years old and Pa made his first visit to Japan after the war. Pa's primary mission was to set up headstones in the village cemetery for Masako and her children. After much investigation, he was able to locate the paternal grandparents who had stolen the child. Pa paid them a social call in Nagoya, where they were still living.

It might be surprising to us that a person who has lived in a certain place as an adult would still be there sixty or seventy years later, or that a family would live in the same house for multiple generations. But this was not uncommon in Japan until recently. We in the United States take mobility for granted; in Japan, things have been more static, especially in rural areas where it had been the expected and usual pattern.

I remember Pa saying to me in the 1950s regarding his home village, "The Tanakas live in that house

Masako's oldest child, and my father's oldest grandchild, Katsumi Murai, in about 1949 (Asai family collection)

next to my nephew's house." I asked, "Did you go there in 1949 on your last trip to visit that family?" His reply was, "No, I didn't, but I would expect that the property has not changed hands. The Tanakas have *always* lived there."

When I visited Pa's childhood home in 1958 myself, I checked up on the neighboring house, and sure enough, the Tanakas were living there, just as they had when my father was a boy. Of course, the current Tanakas did not know Pa, since they were the grand-children or great-grandchildren of the people he had known.

Masako's kidnapped son, Katsumi, never knew his paternal grandparents (the ones who had stolen him from my sister as an infant). The grandfather was ashamed of his part in the whole affair and behaved hospitably to Pa in 1949, but the grandmother was unrepentant. As soon as she learned the identity of her guest, she left the room—an extremely rude gesture, according to Japanese custom. Pa was able to obtain from the man the name and address of the people who had adopted Katsumi.

Pa made a special trip to Tsuruga City (on the west coast of Japan, northwest of Nagoya and due east of South Korea) to find his first grandson. Upon arrival, he learned that the childless couple had divorced, and the man had remarried and was currently living with a woman who had borne him several children. Katsumi was at school when Pa arrived, and the father did not want to reveal the truth to the boy at that time. The facts had been shielded from the boy all those years, mostly because of the social stigma attached to being an adopted child. In Japan, an adopted child often suffers ridicule, much like what the children of unmarried parents faced in American society until the late twentieth century. The boy did not know about his background, and his adoptive father did not wish it to be revealed until such time as it would be impossible to keep it a secret any longer.

The adoptive father was willing, however, to call the boy home from school and disclose the truth if his "American grandfather" insisted upon it. Pa said many times later: "He's my grandson, but he is this man's son. Mr. Murai has been this boy's father for many years; therefore, I have no right to come in and upset things."

Pa left Japan without setting eyes on his grandson. He was 69 years old at the time of his postwar visit to Tsuruga, and he came back to Oregon with a worried look on his face. He was afraid he might not live long enough ever to meet his oldest grandchild—the firstborn of his deceased eldest daughter Masako. One can imagine how difficult it must have been for him to accede to the foster father's wishes.

Pa left money with the parents to have the boy's picture taken and sent to him in America. He began writing letters to Katsumi.

Pa sent him boxes of used clothing and shoes that had been out-grown by the family in Oregon. Often the boy would not see the entire package, only a garment or two from it, as evidenced by his thank-you letters.

As the years went by, Katsumi must have suspected something more than friendship of this relationship. Why would an old man in America want to write letters to a young boy? He began posing many questions about our family, both to Pa and to his adoptive grandfather. He imagined seeing physical similarities between his "father" and the pictures of my brothers, between whom there was no blood relationship.

Finally, when Katsumi completed high school, he applied to work with the post office. When one applies for a job in Japan, one must produce a birth certificate. It was at this time that he learned of his biological father and mother, a fact that his foster fa-ther knew would have to be divulged. After learning of his origins, Katsumi Murai met all his blood relatives in Japan for the first time. The revelation at the age of 17 or 18 was such a shock that it made him an extremely cautious person, not given to trusting words that anyone else might readily accept.

Pa felt a deep responsibility for the future happiness of this boy, who was an orphan in Pa's eyes. His foster father did not have the means to give Katsumi a higher education. Job opportunities be-ing worse in postwar Japan than in the United States at that point, the more education one had, the more opportunity one had to earn something better than subsistence wages.

Pa sent Katsumi monthly allotments to enable him to attend night school. The only stipulation Pa made was that Katsumi had to send a monthly accounting of the money. This went on for a while, but eventually the monthly accountings stopped. Pa learned by communicating with the school that Katsumi was no longer attending it. The boy had suffered from malnutrition during the war and postwar years, and his health was not the best. Working all day in the post office and going to school at night, plus trying to fit in study and sleep, was too much for his frail body to take. He had quietly dropped out of school and not told Pa.

My father was disappointed by the boy's failure to let him know what had happened, and for a brief time Pa quit writing letters to Katsumi, but not until after he had written a bitter letter of anger and disappointment. Throughout all this, Pa could only feel un-happiness that things had turned out as they had.

In 1957-58, I received a Fulbright grant to teach English as a foreign language in Japan. This was an opportunity to meet my nephew. I would be the first member of our family to do so. My meeting with Katsumi occurred in Nagoya, where his paternal grandparents had lived, the city where his mother had died in the war, and where he was now employed as a post office clerk.

At the time, Katsumi was 19 years old. I, his aunt, was 25 and the youngest of the children of his late mother's family in the United States. Although Katsumi had studied English in middle school and high school as required of all Japanese students, he could un-derstand little English spoken by a native and could speak even less and with great difficulty. Fortunately, I could speak enough Japanese to communicate fairly well with him. He did not know this before my arrival and must surely have been nervous about our meeting.

Although I had cousins on my father's side in Nagoya with whom I usually stayed, on this occasion I did not go there. Instead, Katsumi, who worked in the central post office near the railway station, asked me to meet him at work when I arrived in Nagoya. So I did. Katsumi had arranged for the two of us to stay at the Yusei Kaikan, a hotel or inn especially for postal service employees.

Katsumi was tall by Japanese standards. He was good-looking and bore himself proudly, though he was humble in the typical Japanese manner. Shy, reserved, and deferential, he had a look of seriousness coupled with a worried expression. He treated me more as a respected, revered teacher and foreign guest than as an aunt. Although he must surely have been bursting with questions to ask me, he only spoke when I spoke, answered my questions, and responded to what I had to say.

Katsumi maintained this distance with me through my second visit with him eight years later, in 1965, when I met his fiancée, Tatsumi. It was not until 1975, when my hus-

I met my oldest nephew, Katsumi, in Japan in 1957 (Mitzi Loftus)

band Don and I stayed in his home, that he relaxed and broke down the stiff and formal wall between us. Perhaps he had felt beholden to his American family, but by 1975 he had a home with which to offer his hospitality as a proper host, and a wife and children to share.

For that first meeting with Katsumi in 1957, I brought a message from Pa inviting his grandson to come to America at my father's expense and attend a university. When I told Katsumi this, to my surprise his reply was that he would have to think it over. On my next encounter with him, he told me that he could not accept. I asked him why, and his answer was something like this.

"I cannot handle the English language now. If I went to America, perhaps I could pick up the language; however, even with facility in English, I might not be able to handle the academic load at the university. If your father goes to the expense of bringing me to the United States and of sending me to college, and then I should fail,

I could not bear the weight of that much responsibility. I will take my chances by staying in Japan instead." I knew that my father would be disappointed, so I tried to get Katsumi to reconsider, but he was definite in his decision.

My fiancé Don Loftus had been teaching school in Oregon while I was teaching in Shizuoka, Japan. He flew to Tokyo in June 1958 for our marriage. We had a wedding dinner and invited all my fellow Fulbright teachers, my host family from Kambara-Machi, a few old friends who were living in Tokyo, and Katsumi. He was our guest at International House.

This was his first view of Tokyo and likely his first experience of staying in a Western-style hotel; that is, sleeping on a bed instead of on the floor. Katsumi was to make many subsequent trips to Tokyo over the years, however, as various opportunities opened for him through the post office. During training for the foreign department of the post office, he studied English and French at the Post Office Employees' Academy.

I corresponded with Katsumi between 1958 and 1965 while I lived in Eugene. Sometimes we would correspond in English, sometimes in French, but we have never written to each other in Japanese. My parents were able to go to Japan together in 1960 and meet Katsumi themselves. In the summer of 1965, I made a vacation trip back to Japan, taking with me our first child, David, who had just turned 6 in March.

Before I left the United States on that trip, Pa came to Eugene from Hood River. He was excited about having received a letter from Katsumi regarding his possible marriage. Katsumi wanted Pa to come to the wedding in the spring of 1966. If that were not possible, he wished to marry that winter. Pa told me to be sure to meet the girl his oldest grandson intended to marry. He didn't say so, but I think he was worried Katsumi was about to marry someone inappropriate. So it became my task to approve of Tatsumi to become Katsumi's wife.

On this visit, once again in Nagoya, I stayed at my cousin's house. My cousin and her son's family had a flourishing business in the towel and bedclothes business, with a main store in Nagoya and a branch in Tokyo. They arranged for a nice dinner at their home for us, and invited Katsumi and Tatsumi. There were only three of us around the table, plus a visiting cousin from the country, a young man about Katsumi's age. My hostess cousin bustled in and out, serving us the way a Japanese hostess does in such cases. She was helped in these duties by her daughter-in-law, Sumiko, who along with her family lived under the same roof.

Tatsumi was shy and treated me with the same deference as did Katsumi, speaking only when spoken to. Tatsumi had some higher education and was working as a secretary in a firm in Nagoya—I believe in the import-export business. She had of course studied English but did not admit to being able to understand or speak it. In later years, I received several letters from her, written in her hand and in English.

On this occasion, however, she kept her head lowered, her hands in her lap, the perfect picture of what a young Japanese prospective bride should be. My cousin related details of Katsumi's early childhood years to Tatsumi, in case she had not heard them. My cousin said, "Katsumi is an orphan and has had some hard years growing up, so we must all work together to make the rest of his life happy."

Upon hearing this, Tatsumi wept softly. My cousin was impressed with Tatsumi's gentle, sympathetic personality, and I agreed with her that Tatsumi seemed very sweet and would make a fine wife and addition to the family. I tried to think what Grandmother Asai, who had arranged for Pa's bride, would feel about this girl. Most of the time, I believe, your first impression of a person is generally correct. And as the years have gone by, I could see that she was everything I guessed she would be.

I told Pa that Tatsumi would be fine for Katsumi, and the arrangements for the wedding began. Pa planned to attend. Ma did not go with Pa to Japan because of her health. The doctor would not permit her to fly. Ma did not wish to go anyway; the only reason she had gone in 1960 was because Pa and the family pressed her to go. Every relative of hers that I visited asked me, "Why doesn't your mother come to see us? We want to see her again." I had to tell them that she did not want to return to Japan.

We had talked about the possibility many times. Each time, her response was the same: "I said goodbye once, and I don't want to say goodbye again. I hate partings. My family and my life is now here in the US. I don't need to go back to Japan. Besides, there are too many insects there, it's too humid, and I don't like to sleep on the floor." Because of her 1942 injury from falling down the stairs while packing for the camps, a bed on the floor was torture to her. When she finally went to Japan in 1960 under duress, she came home grumbling about the dirty Japanese toilets and the uncomfortable sleeping arrangements. She had become used to sitting on a flush toilet; squatting over a hole in the floor was too uncomfortable for a person her age and condition.

Pa wanted to buy or build a house for the couple, so Katsumi could more easily support a family as a postal clerk. Now that marriage figured into the picture, Pa could see that at last the unfinished business of his orphaned grandson could be taken care of. In the spring of 1966, at age 86, Pa traveled alone to Japan, and on land given to the young couple by Tatsumi's parents, he had a prefabricated house built.

Pa was very proud of this house. He told all his Japanese relatives about its dimensions: "It is five mats long and has three rooms plus a kitchen." The Japanese did not use inches and feet or metric measurements to tell the size of a room or house in those days; instead, they referred to the number of tatami mats a home could hold. A tatami mat is made of rice straw and bound around the edges with brocade cloth. Tatami are typically the size of an American bed but half the width, so the five mats my father boasted of would have been maybe ten by fifteen feet, small for an American room. Three to five inches thick and set down into the recessed floor, tatami are pleasant to walk on in one's bare or stockinged feet and act as a cushion under the quilt pads laid on the floor for beds at night.

In a traditional Japanese home, the living room becomes a dining room with the simple addition of a small, low table around which the diners sit on the floor. When evening comes, the table is removed, the quilts are laid on the floor, and the room becomes a bedroom.

For the young newlywed couple, the prefabricated home my father gifted them was a magnificent beginning. Most couples in that era would live either with their parents or in a crowded apartment for some years. When the house was finished, Pa moved into it along with Katsumi. The two of them lived there for a couple of weeks before the wedding took place.

When Pa left Japan, Katsumi and Tatsumi accompanied him on the several-hours-long train ride to Tokyo to see him off. It was dusk when Pa boarded the plane at Haneda International Airport, a little bent figure, 86 years old and barely five feet tall, traveling alone. Katsumi wrote that his wife sobbed uncontrollably as she watched Pa climb the steps into the plane that was to take him away from them, probably forever. This was related to Pa in a letter from Katsumi, which he shared with us many times.

Although he had to return in haste to America, due to Ma's failing health, Pa came home with a new look of peace and contentment. It was as though his life work was at last completed.

CHAPTER 14

Fulbright Teacher in Japan

My professional goals had always included plans to go overseas to teach. I was particularly impressed that Senator J. William Fulbright from Arkansas came up with the idea of arranging foreign exchanges of grad students and professors in 1945, just a few days after the atomic bomb was dropped on Japan. Can you imagine the audacity of a politician doing that at the time? He had only been elected to the Senate a year before—and the House a year before that—and this seemingly audacious proposal passed.

I had an idealistic notion that this was the best program to go on. But I knew the competition would be great, and I learned that the Fulbright program was not open to anyone who didn't have at least three years of teaching experience. So I first taught three years at Creswell, and applied in May or June of 1956 for the following school year. If I didn't get the Fulbright, I would go into some other program, just so I could teach abroad.

In my application, I was asked to put three choices of countries where I wished to teach. My greatest desire was to go to a French-speaking country since I had studied French for several years. But my father had taught us, maybe in words or just by example, "Never let your heart rule your head." My heart said I wanted to go to a French-speaking country, but my head told me that I should go to Japan. I could speak the language, and I knew something about the culture. So I put Japan first, even though my heart didn't want to go to Japan. Belgium and Martinique were my second and third choices. (There were no opportunities in France itself that year.)

That summer of 1956 I attended the wedding of a friend, Bob Biggs, in the Waldport-Yachats area of the central Oregon coast. The best man at that wedding was Don Loftus. I rode back to Eugene with Don and Partap Kapoor, an exchange student from Kashmir, India, who had been sponsored in this country by Bob. When I got home, Don said, "Can I pick you up for breakfast?" This was summertime, my first term of graduate work. I told him it would have to be early since I had a class at nine o'clock. He was working nights at a cannery, I think, and got off in the early morning, so we had a breakfast date before he went home to sleep.

Don picked me up for breakfast pretty much every morning that summer. He found out I had applied for a Fulbright and suggested I withdraw my application. I couldn't understand why, since traveling on a Fulbright scholarship was something I'd wanted to do for years. Then, that Christmas, he surprised me with an engagement ring. I told him I wasn't sure I was ready for it. He was undaunted, replying, "Well, will you keep it until you're ready?" So I put it in the glove compartment.

I had a difficult interview for the Fulbright in Portland that winter, when a three-member committee questioned me. One was a professor at one of the universities in Portland who was from Norway or Sweden. I don't remember the second person, but the third was a male professor who asked me searing questions that made me nervous. One of the last was: "I see that you're Japanese American. Where did you spend your time during World War II?" I had worried the committee would ask me that, and I responded, "Well, I was in a camp; my family were all put in camps."

And he asked, "What are you going to tell the Japanese people about that?" I said, "If they don't ask me, I'm not going tell them anything. And if they ask me, I'll tell them the truth." When he asked those questions, I thought, *Well, there go my chances.* To have to tell the Japanese people that I was locked up by the American government during World War II sounded terrible.

By the spring vacation of 1957, I had not heard from the Fulbright Commission, so Don and I announced our engagement. About two weeks after that, I received a letter of acceptance, announcing my grant award and notification of my assignment to teach English in Japan. I think this raised my attitude about the Fulbright program even more. If they knew this about me and still let me go, it was a point in favor of the Fulbright.

The irony was, I didn't want to go to Japan because I was still suffering from a somewhat subconscious but firm rejection of my Japanese heritage. I was dismayed that I had been accepted and was going to be sent to Japan. But I wanted to go anywhere rather than nowhere. I didn't want to go abroad just to teach; I wanted to learn a culture and get the whole cultural experience, no matter where I went.

For a couple of months, I anguished over the decision. Should I go to Japan, which would necessitate a yearlong engagement period apart? Should I turn down the grant and get married? I decided that in all fairness to myself and to the future of our marriage, I should go to Japan. I did not want to catch myself in later years blaming Don, saying amidst some domestic quarrel: "If I hadn't married you, I could have gone to Japan to teach English!"

That summer before my departure, I attended the English Language Institute of the University of Michigan in Ann Arbor to receive training for teaching English as a foreign language. This requirement was paid for by the US State Department. The students were from all over; my roommate was from Baghdad, Iraq, and my best friend was a girl from Chile. The most interesting students were a group of Cubans. We were not supposed to speak anything but English at the institute, but in private they chattered away in Spanish. A letter would come to them from home, and they'd weep. I didn't understand what was going on; I just thought they were emotional Latins. It wasn't until years later that I realized this was during the Cuban Revolution, when Castro was coming to power.

The training was wonderful. I learned a lot, not only how to teach effectively in Japan, but also how to teach French in American schools in the sixties, and later English as a Second Language to people from many foreign places. From 1979 until 2009, I taught ESL at Southwestern Oregon Community College and had more than 250 students from at least forty countries with twenty-two different language backgrounds.

I arrived at my host family's house in Kambara—a town five stations down the main Tokaido rail line from Shizuoka City, where I would be teaching—after dark and found a big dinner waiting for me. The dean of the School of Education, several English professors from Shizuoka University, the principal of the middle school where I was assigned to teach that year, my host, and I sat at the table. They were all men. The ladies of the house (Mrs. Yabuuchi, her daughter, and the maid) bustled about serving us. After dinner, the men excused themselves and went home, having recognized that I was tired and needed to retire as soon as possible.

I was ushered into the rooms I would occupy for the year. They were Japanese-style rooms with tatami mats. As soon as Mrs. Yabuuchi, her daughter Miye, and the servant reached the doorway of my rooms, they knelt, as they would the entire year I was there. In the American-style rooms, this was not necessary, but when one approached Japanese-style rooms, Japanese customs ruled.

In Japanese custom, one must not place one's head or body equal to or higher than an honored person or one considered higher

My host family's daughter, Miye, and me during my Fulbright year, 1957–58 (Mitzi Loftus)

in social rank. I was the honored American teacher, to whom a kneeling posture meant one was paying proper respect. A few times their 13-year-old daughter came to my room to ask me a question and failed to kneel. If her mother had been anywhere nearby, it would have warranted a severe reprimand.

I entered my room followed by three ladies scooting in after me, on their knees. They began to help me get undressed. I was not prepared for this and stiffened slightly. The daughter said, "Mother, perhaps she would rather not have us do this." Her mother replied, "Nonsense—we're all women."

So I gulped and allowed myself to be "served." Then I followed the servant down the stairs to the bath. She came into the bath and scrubbed my back. I told her that was fine and excused her, but I noticed she was waiting for me in the outer dressing area. I opened the sliding opaque glass doors and repeated to her that I no longer needed her services. She nodded but stayed there until I finished bathing and dressing so that she could accompany me back up the stairs. It was not until quite some time later that I understood what a difficult position I had put her in. She was ordered by her mistress and lady of the house to stay with me. Then she was dismissed by me as being of unnecessary service. She was caught in between, trying to serve two mistresses.

Remember the Hachiya family, divided in half because Mrs. Hachiya was so homesick she took her son Homer back to Japan and left the other son Frank (who would be killed in action in the Philippines) in Hood River with her husband? By the time I was in Japan on my Fulbright, Homer was married and living in Yokohama, so I visited him there. Mrs. Hachiya lived in a small town near Okayama, and when I went there to see her, I was still her little girl. She would have been in her forties then. She said, "I want to give you something, but I don't have anything proper. I'd like to give you this necklace, although it's kind of for an old person." I love that necklace, made of tiny mother of pearl, and I still wear it sometimes.

When I was in Japan, Don called me several times. I was so worried about the cost of using the telephone long distance, I wouldn't respond to his questions, and he'd say, "Mitzi, are you there?" He wrote me a letter just about every day. Don was teaching music in Bethel District schools, at the north end of Eugene, that year. At the end of the 1957-58 school year of teaching at Shizuoka University School of Education and its Attached Middle School, Don flew to meet me in Tokyo, where we were married on June 17, 1958. Our marriage ceremony consisted of signing a few papers at the Tokyo American Consulate and at the Japanese Ward Office (office of city hall).

At six feet, three inches, and with pale white skin from his Norwegian/northern European background, Don presented a visual contrast to my even five feet. My sister and older brothers all married other Nisei until Gene, the second brother above me (or the fifth child in Asai family birth order). In 1953, Gene married outside the Japanese American community and didn't tell our parents for a whole year. I think he feared that if he had told them ahead of time, my parents would disapprove of the match, and

With my new husband Don Loftus, in the sun room at the Yabuuchis', my host family in Kambara, Japan, June 1958 (Mitzi Loftus)

then he would have married Barbara anyway and had to deal with that. So he married her first, told my folks a year later, and then they had to get used to the idea. But that made it easier for me a few more years down the road.

I still had teaching obligations, so we returned to Shizuoka City, where we stayed at the Nakashimaya Inn while I finished out the week of school. Then we returned to Tokyo for the weekend, where I had arranged for a wedding dinner in a Chinese restaurant, attended by all the Fulbright teachers, some members of the Fulbright Commission in Japan, my nephew Katsumi, my host father and sister, and a few other friends living in Tokyo—perhaps twenty-five to thirty persons.

Imagine our surprise when we cut the wedding cake and brown crumbs came up with the knife! I had ordered the cake but had not specified a white cake, assuming that a wedding cake would automatically be made traditional white. But not in Japan. It was a delicious spice cake, much better than what I could have planned.

Don and I then flew to the northern island of Hokkaido for a week's honeymoon and toured the Ainu village of Shiraoi, the fabulous hot spring resort of Noboribetsu with its *senninburo* (a bath that accommodates a thousand bathers), and Lake Toya.

We returned from our honeymoon in Hokkaido by train, traveling from north to south on the main island of Honshu. Don stuck around because he was on his summer break, but I returned to my teaching duties in Shizuoka. In July, there was a weeklong national English teachers' seminar at International Christian University in Tokyo. Two teachers were selected from each prefecture to attend it. Don and I stayed in the dormitories in that humid heat of Tokyo in July, while all of us Fulbright teachers served as instructors at this seminar.

After the seminar was over, I traveled south to visit my relatives in Iwata, Toyohashi, Nagoya, and Yatomi, this time for Don to meet them. We continued south to Ise Peninsula to view the national Shinto shrines and Mikimoto's Pearl Island. From there we went to Osaka and continued the second part of our honeymoon by ferrying to the Inland Sea from Akashi to the island of Shikoku.

We took the train across the island of Shikoku from Takamatsu to Matsuyama and ferried to Hiroshima back on the island of Honshu. There we visited the Peace Museum, erected at the spot where the first atomic bomb was dropped. Our intention was to see the southern island of Kyushu, but the heat and humidity of August in that semitropical region were too oppressive. The last week we spent in Japan we climbed Mt. Fuji in the company of another young couple, both of whom were teachers. By that time, I was pregnant with my first son David. My morning sickness was so bad I vomited into the crater.

We came from such different cultural backgrounds and home environments. I tried to explain to Don that I came from a non-verbal culture. We don't express feelings, neither anger nor love, with words. He asked, "Well, how do you know?" I said, "You either love or you hate, and the person's gonna know it from your behavior. And if you don't get it nonverbally, you'll never get it."

He didn't get it for a *long* time. At the end of my Fulbright year in Japan, Don picked me up in San Francisco and we went directly to Hood River to see my parents. I walked in the house, right up to my parents who were sitting at the table. They didn't especially smile, and they didn't scowl; it was as if I had just stepped out to get a stick of wood for the stove. No expression whatsoever, and no reference to feelings. My father asked how our flight was. He then asked if we'd like something to eat, and how long the trip was from San Francisco.

Afterward, Don said, "My god, you were gone five thousand miles for a whole year, and they acted like you just went to the corner grocery store and came back!"

I said, "That's what so wonderful about my cultural background. You know exactly where you stand with each other, and you take up just where you left off. It doesn't matter how much time and how many miles you are apart; you don't worry about the past or future, or ask what are you going to do now to please me or make me unhappy or angry." Don came from a huggy-kissy family that said a lot, but there wasn't a lot of true meaning behind it. I hear people say, "I love you," especially on the telephone, waiting for the other person to say, "I love you, too." To me, that has no meaning at all; it's something you say because you want the response and expect it. And that's a hard thing to explain to people.

He chided me one time. He said, "You need to hug the boys more." And I said, "If I did that, they would be startled. They would say, what's happened to Mom? They know your style, and they know my style, and they're completely different—but they know what the messages are. If you went silent, they would be surprised, or maybe amazed, and if I did like you do, then they would also wonder what had happened."

In August 1958, we were back in Oregon, where we would live in Eugene for the next eleven years. Our first son David was born in 1959, the year of statehood for Don's home state, Alaska. During that first year of marriage and pregnancy I took university classes, working toward completing my master's degree, while Don taught music at Thomas Jefferson Junior High School. When David was 6 months old, I took a two-thirds-time position as a French teacher at Wilson Junior High, while Don took the year off from teaching to pursue a master's degree in piano performance. He gave private piano lessons at home while studying at the university and taking piano lessons himself.

After my year as a French teacher, I did secondary substitute teaching for a few years. At the same time, I opened a tropical fish shop at the front of our house at 1409 Oak Street. As the Evergreen Aquarium business grew, I found it impossible to continue substituting. For nine years, this business occupied most of my time, in addition to the arrival of our second son, Kenneth, in 1964. Ourc third son, Toby, was born in 1968.

I received my MA in June 1962. During 1964-65, I served as a graduate assistant in the School of Education at the University of Oregon as a supervisor of student teachers of French. I traveled to many high schools each week in the Eugene-Springfield area, to observe student teachers in action and to act as a liaison between them and their supervising teachers and schools. I can remember earning nine hundred dollars for this position, which helped finance the trip to Japan in the summer of 1965. David went with me after finishing kindergarten and before entering first grade. This was the trip during which I approved the prospective bride of my nephew, Katsumi (related in chapter 13).

On the Hood River fruit orchard of my birth, my eldest brother Tot reared four children. Three daughters attended his alma mater, Oregon State, and his son attended the University of Oregon. His eldest daughter Marta and her husband Phil, both pharmacists, later returned to Hood River to share in the operation of the fruit orchards. They raised two daughters very near to the original Asai house so all three generations have continued close relations, just as my parents did.

Pa and Ma lived with Tot and his growing family in the same household until their deaths in 1967 and 1969. Tot's children are the only grandchildren who had the daily benefit of hearing and speaking Japanese with their grandparents. It is amazing how small children can distinguish one language from another without being instructed. When Marta was about 3 years old, she suddenly realized that soy sauce was always called *shoyu* in our house and that that was not English. "What's the English word for *shoyu*?" she demanded.

At an early age, she once asked Grandma to read her a story. Ma said, "Sorry, Marta. No can read." Marta looked puzzled for a moment, then said, "Then why don't you put on your gwasses?" Grandma had to admit that even with her glasses on, she could not read. Marta consoled her with "that's all wight, Gwandma. You can do LOTS of things."

Pa went to Japan in 1966 for the wedding of Katsumi and Tatsumi. He had intended to stay in Japan afterward to do some traveling, but soon after he left Oregon, Ma became ill. While Pa was gone, Ma's blood pressure rose and stayed up. I concluded that it was worry that caused her condition. It seemed important for Pa to come home. No one had told him about Ma; it was kept from him so as not to spoil his travel plans. I wrote to him that if the wedding were over and all the important things were done, he should return home, for Ma was ill. He dropped everything and came home, and the next year, Ma died at the age of 74.

Ma had had eight healthy children but worked long hours and days for many years. As a result, she had an enlarged heart, much like that of an athlete, which the doctor said came from her early years working so hard physically. High blood pressure plagued her final years. The night before she died, Ma enjoyed a gathering with friends who shared pictures they had taken of a trip together to Yellowstone Park. The next day, she walked to the mailbox at noon to get the mail and fell down behind the mailboxes. She died of a heart attack and was found later in the orchard. At the time of Ma's death, I was 34 years old. Since I was the youngest of the family, one could say that all eight children had grown to maturity by then, although Masako and Half had died long before.

In 1968, Pa made a final trip to Japan, this time with Mika. His eyesight and hearing were showing signs of his age (88), and it was a great relief to the family that he did not go alone this time, as he had done in 1966. The two of them enjoyed Katsumi's hospitality and that of his wife, Tatsumi, in the house that had been built two years earlier by Pa. On this visit, Pa bought a washing machine, which was undoubtedly a help when the young couple had two children.

For Mika, it was an emotional visit because she, more than anyone else in the family, resembled Masako, Katsumi's mother. All the relatives wept when she appeared, for she seemed to be a face out of the past to them. Hearing this, Katsumi would gaze in silence at Mika's face for long periods, wondering and imagining if this was what his mother looked like—the mother he never knew.

Pa died in February 1969, a year after his final visit to Japan, just a short time after celebrating his eighty-ninth birthday. Our youngest son Toby had celebrated his first birthday in January. Pa, Masako, Dick, Don, Kenneth, and Toby were all born in the month of January—a good month.

In the meantime, a daughter was born to Katsumi and Tatsumi in Japan. She was named Mitsuko, after me, the first American relative Katsumi had met. I was able to see Katsumi again when Don and I went to Japan on a "second honeymoon" in 1975. We were Katsumi's guests in his house in Jimokuji. There I played *pachinko*, a kind of Japanese pinball machine, with Mitsuko, who was then

5 years old. By this time she had a little brother, Katsuichiro, four years younger than she.

Pa with a prize mushroom find in the late 1940s
(Asai family collection)

Epilogue

My generation, the Nisei born in this country of Japanese immigrant Issei parents, is almost gone now. Most of the Nisei who were taken to the camps never talked about the experience afterward out of shame and fear. James and Toshi Nagamori Ito, who met in the Heart Mountain camp, were typical of our generation: their son Lance Ito said they never mentioned it at home. Only after she retired from her postwar career as an elementary school teacher in the Los Angeles Unified School District did his mother write an article about her camp experience in a local newsletter. Challenged and called a liar, she felt compelled to write and publish a memoir with the subtitle "U.S.A. Concentration Camp Inmate, War Bride, Mother of Chrisie and Judge Lance Ito."[1]

My family also never liked to talk about it. I think the rest of my family were typically Japanese, not wanting to dwell on negative things. As a Zen Buddhist, my father believed negative emotions like regret, anger, guilt, and sadness destroy you if you dwell on them.

I was young enough, and American enough, that I talked about my experiences in public soon after the war. College classmates may have asked questions. My first public talk was probably in the late 1950s, at First Christian Church in Eugene, or maybe Creswell High, where I first taught school. By the early 1970s, I regularly spoke to students at North Bend High and Marshfield High on the southern coast of Oregon, where I taught as a substitute. I gave talks to the general public in Coos County maybe ten times: at the Coos Bay Public Library, Myrtle Point Library, churches in Coquille, Southwestern Oregon Community College, and in Florence and Brookings in the adjoining counties.

Since the turn of the millennium, I've given similar speeches in Klamath Falls, Oregon, and Redding, California; at libraries, colleges, Unitarian-Universalist fellowships, and chapters of the League of Women Voters. The online *Oregon Encyclopedia* project, on whose board I served, formed a partnership with the McMenamins chain of brewpubs and hotels to present history talks, and I've done nearly a dozen of those in Portland, McMinnville, and Bend. All told, I've spoken publicly about the camp experience and racism against my family roughly fifty times.

I've learned over the years that it was a well-kept secret from people it didn't concern. Every time I speak, someone comes forward and says, "You know, I had this very good friend in school who was Japanese, and suddenly they disappeared and we didn't know where they went." I don't know how many times I've heard that from different people, which means there was a concerted effort to keep it hidden because people in power knew it wasn't the right thing to do—and they were doing something that was probably not constitutionally legal.

Now, as then, people will say, "It was to protect you. It was for your own protection." But nobody asked us what we wanted. We didn't ask to be protected. We might have taken our chances and stayed home to see what happened to us. We'd have chosen that over being locked up for three years. Wouldn't you?

After many years of lobbying from the Japanese American community, Congress passed the Civil Liberties Act of 1988, which said the whole World War II "evacuation" was wrong, the nation owed its citizens an apology, and the United States ought to pay reparations. Any person who lived in the camps was to receive

$20,000. My mother and father were owed that money, but by 1988 they were dead. My brothers had been in the army, so they didn't receive any reparations. People like me, a happy kid playing in the camps with her neighbors, did receive the $20,000 payment. A friend who was a social studies teacher at a high school where I taught asked his classes, "How many of you would be willing to give up your civil rights, and be locked up for three years, for $20,000?" Nobody raised his hand; even high school teenagers decades after the war didn't go for it.

When 9/11 happened, a Japanese exchange student happened to be staying in my home. I said, "Just you wait. The same thing's gonna happen to the Muslims and the Arab folks in this country." She looked as if to say, *What are you talking about?* And I said, "It won't be too long; maybe in about three months." It took only two weeks, maybe, before some American citizens started to talk about "locking 'em up."

Especially when I talk to high school kids about my camp experience and afterward, I say, "It was not Mrs. Bettsworth and the dog who hurt me. It's the good people who knew when something was wrong and never said or did anything. There were many people who befriended us in private, when there was nobody else around, but if they saw you next day in town, in public, they didn't recognize you. That's what most people do; that's about 98 percent of people. That other 2 percent needs to grow. When a kid is bullied in your class, or in your school, how many people stand up and say, 'Quit that! You're mean!'? But you have to do that. If you don't, this is what happens."

More than thirty years have passed since a version of this book was published. Today, our family has slimmed down to just me. My sister Mika passed away in November 2022 at the age of 99, and I am now 91. The youngest of my five brothers, Dick, died first in

1993 at age 64; the two eldest, Tot and Min, both died at age 85; and brother number four, Gene, died at 85 in 2012. My niece and nephews carry on in Hood River, tending the orchards my father started so many years ago. (If he were living today, he would be 144 years old.)

As for my own family, in the summer of 1969, Don and I drove our three sons in a Volkswagen bus we had converted into a camper across the United States en route to Europe. On our way, we stopped at the site of Heart Mountain camp. There was nothing to see except for an abandoned barrack; no historic marker or sign. It was a little sad to find an empty field where I had lived for two years in "Wyoming's third-largest city" barely twenty-five years before.

Fifty years after that visit, however, Heart Mountain had a beautiful interpretive center, with photos and detailed captions. It's possibly the most informative facility of all the former incarceration camp sites today, even the infamous one at Tule Lake. Funds are being raised to fix the massive root cellar where stacks of winter vegetables were stored for the detainees, and to make it safe for visitors to walk through.[2] Former NBC news anchor and author Tom Brokaw interviewed me briefly for his video notebook during a 2019 gathering at Heart Mountain. He declared that every person who runs for public office should be required to visit Heart Mountain and learn its history.

After my husband Don died as the result of an accident caused by an intoxicated driver in 1996, I lived alone in Coos Bay for nine years, then moved to Ashland, near the California border, to be within walking distance of my son Ken and his family, and the Oregon Shakespeare Festival, which I had attended over many years. My other two sons live in the Portland area.

Before and after my husband's death, I traveled alone to many places. Altogether from that first trip to Japan with my mother in 1935, I have visited Japan about ten times. I remember visiting Mr.

Interviewed by legendary TV anchor Tom Brokaw during the 2019 Heart Mountain Pilgrimage, July 27, 2019 (Toby Loftus)

Hachiya in Okayama, where he settled after decades of living apart from his wife in the United States. He had not wanted to return to Japan; he told me how miserable he was there and died a few short years later. He was one of the few Issei who spoke and wrote good English. My sister Mika and I went together in 1995. While Don was attending a piano tuners' convention in Kyoto, we went to visit Mrs. Hachiya. By then I was more than 60 years old, so she would have to have been over 80.

My hometown of Hood River has changed so much. My dad used to say, "You'll never get rich raising apples, but you will al-ways feed your family." For many years he was correct; I'm glad he died before that was no longer true. Because of economic global-ization, Chinese, Chilean, and New Zealand fruit gets shipped in and sells for cheaper than the fruit my nieces and nephews grow. In some years, my family left the apples on the trees. They also switched to pears and cherries. Today, many former Hood River fruit farms are now wine vineyards. The town has also become the windsurfing capital of the world, drawing athletes from all over to surf the Columbia River Gorge, so I can't find the grocery or hardware shops I used to know. They're all sports and recreation shops now.

In just the past few years, the town of Hood River, the state of Oregon, and the nation have taken further steps to make amends for the harm done to tens of thousands of Japanese American citizens, and to acknowledge the grace with which we responded. The outdoor courts in Oak Grove Park where my oldest brother used to play tennis after the war have been renamed the Taro Asai Tennis Courts. In the summer of 2021, the US Postal Service issued a postage stamp to honor Nisei veterans of World War II like my late brothers. In August 2022, Highway 35, a scenic route up the Hood River Valley from the Columbia River to Mount Hood, was dedicated as the Oregon Nisei Veterans World War II Memorial Highway following a unanimous vote by the Oregon legislature. And as part of its Veterans Day observance in November 2022, the current officers and members of American Legion Post 22 in Hood River made a formal apology to Nisei veterans for the actions of the post during the war that culminated in the honor roll incident. Gary Akiyama, the son of George Akiyama—the veteran who was on that honor roll and was refused service after the war by a barber who said, "I ought to slit your throat"—commented at the ceremony, "Two of the hardest things to do in life are to ask for forgiveness and say, 'sorry, I blew it.' This is a significant move. We are eternally grateful."[3]

The other change is that my family was always known as the "AE-sighs." Nobody pronounced our name the Japanese way, which is "ah-sah-ee." All of my life I was an "AE-sigh" (and Half became "Ace"). When I went to the University of Oregon, I didn't respond to the roll call because the professor pronounced my name correctly!

One of my grand nieces, my nephew Sam's daughter (descendants of my brother Min), became an attorney in Portland. I'd never known her because I left home before these kids grew up. One day I thought, I think I'll go see what her office is like. So I went to the big lobby/reception area of this five- or six-story building in downtown Portland about nine one morning and asked, "Has Jessica AE-sigh arrived yet?" The concierge gave me this stern look and said, "You mean Ah-sah-ee?" I said, "Yeah, that one."

So things have changed a little.

Notes

CHAPTER I

1. American Field Service, *AFS-USA Fact Sheet,* Lit. No. 13003 (New York: AFS, 2013), https://www.acpsmd.org/cms/lib/MD01907365/Centricity/Domain/27/AFS%20Fact%20Sheet.pdf.

CHAPTER 2

1 "List or Manifest of Alien Passengers for the U.S. Immigration Officer at Port of Arrival," List H(1), May 23, 1904, retrieved May 15, 2016 from Ancestry.com.

2 "Edison Film Coptic," search results from the Library of Congress, accessed July 30, 2023, https://www.loc.gov/search/?in=&q=Edison+film+Coptic&new=true&st=.

3 Nicholas J. Evans, "Indirect Passage: Transmigration via the UK, 1836-1914," *Journal for Maritime Research* 3, no. 1 (June 2001): https://www.tandfonline.com/doi/abs/10.1080/21533369.2001.9668313.

4 "The Germans in America," European Reading Room, April 23, 2014, https://www.loc.gov/rr/european/imde/germchro.html.

5 Masako Herman, *The Japanese in America 1843-1973* (Dobbs Ferry, NY: Oceana Publications, 1974), 2. Sean Yoshikawa, "Imagining Home: Stories of Exile and Migration in the San Francisco Bay Area," CCSF Oral History Project, January 2016, https://ccsforalhistoryproject.wordpress.com/2015/12/23/249/comment-page-1/.

6 "Naturalization Act of 1870," Encyclopedia.com, accessed July 30, 2023, https://www.encyclopedia.com/humanities/applied-and-social-sciences-magazines/naturalization-act-1870.

7 Franklin Odo, "Alien Land Laws in California (1913 & 1920)," Immigration and Ethnic History Society, University of Texas at

Austin, accessed July 30, 2023, https://immigrationhistory.org/item/alien-land-laws-in-california-1913-1920/.

8   Jacqueline Peterson-Loomis, "Immigration and Exclusion Time Line, Oregon History 101," *Oregon Encyclopedia*, accessed July 30, 2023, https://www.oregonencyclopedia.org/media/uploads/Oregon_History_101_Timeline_12-1-14.pdf.

9   Brian Niiya, "California Joint Immigration Committee," Densho Encyclopedia, last updated April 18, 2014, https://encyclopedia.densho.org/California_Joint_Immigration_Committee/.

10 "The Immigration Act of 1924 (the Johnson-Reed Act)," Office of the Historian, Foreign Service Institute, US Department of State, accessed July 30, 2023, https://history.state.gov/milestones/1921-1936/immigration-act.

11 Franklin Odo, *The Columbia Documentary History of the Asian American Experience* (New York: Columbia University Press, 2002); as cited in "Immigration and Nationality Act of 1952 (McCarran-Walter Act)," Immigration History: A Project of the Immigration and Ethnic History Society, Department of History, University of Texas at Austin, accessed May 24, 2023, https://immigrationhistory.org/item/immigration-and-nationality-act-the-mccarran-walter-act/.

12 "Immigration and Nationality Act of 1965," History, Art & Archives, US House of Representatives, October 3, 1965, https://history.house.gov/Historical-Highlights/1951-2000/Immigration-and-Nationality-Act-of-1965/.

13 "Thirteenth Census of the United States: 1910—Population," State Oregon, County Hood River, South Hood River Precinct, Department of Commerce and Labor—Bureau of the Census, Sheet No. 4B, retrieved from Ancestry.com, May 15, 2016.

14 "Fourteenth Census of the United States: 1920—Population," State Oregon, County Hood River, Oak Grove Precinct, Department of Commerce and Labor—Bureau of the Census, Sheet No. 10A, retrieved from Ancestry.com, May 15, 2016.

15 "List or Manifest of Alien Passengers for the U.S. Immigration Officer at Port of Arrival," July 19, 1911, retrieved from Ancestry.com, May 15, 2016.

16 Manifest No. 2750-18, August 3, 1911, retrieved from Ancestry.com, May 15, 2016.

17 Marriage Certificate, State of Washington, County of King, No. 31938, August 4, 1911, filed September 1, 1911, retrieved from Ancestry.com, March 6, 2017.

CHAPTER 3

1 "List or Manifest of Alien Passengers for the U.S. Immigration Officer at Port of Arrival," February 13, 1916, retrieved from Ancestry.com, May 15, 2016.

2 Port of Seattle cards, Manifest nos. 5950-8 and 5950-9, March 1, 1916, retrieved from Ancestry.com, May 15, 2016.

CHAPTER 6

1 "Historic Columbia River Highway State Trail," State of Oregon website, accessed August 1, 2023, https://www.oregon.gov/odot/regions/pages/state-trail.aspx.

2 Masuo Yasui, "Letter from Masuo Yasui to Sagoro Asai, 1946 January 18," Coll 956, Folder 2, Oregon Historical Society Research Library, accessed August 1, 2023, https://digitalcollections.ohs.org/coll-956-masuo-yasui-letter-to-sagoro-asai-1946-january-18.

CHAPTER 7

1 James C. McNaughton, "Japanese Americans and the U.S. Army," *Army History* 59 (Summer-Fall 2003): 11, cited in Brian Niiya, "Japanese Americans in Military during World War II," Densho Encyclopedia, last updated January 26, 2023. https://encyclopedia.densho.org/Japanese_Americans_in_military_during_World_War_II/.

2 Donald R. McCoy and Richard T. Ruetten, *Quest and Response: Minority Rights and the Truman Administration* (Lawrence: University Press of Kansas, 1973), 4.

3 "Japanese-American Soldiers in WW2 Served While Losing Their Rights," VeteranLife, accessed August 3, 2023, https://veteranlife.com/military-history/japanese-american-soldiers-in-ww2/.

4 "Hood River Community Hall, 1929," photo from Takagi Family Collection, Oregon Nikkei Legacy Center, Discover Nikkei: Japanese Migrants and Their Descendants, accessed August 3, 2023, https://discovernikkei.org/en/nikkeialbum/albums/202/slide/?page=10.

5 Office of the Historian, Foreign Service Institute, United States Department of State, "The Immigration and Nationality Act of 1952 (The McCarran-Walter Act)," accessed August 30, 2023, https://history.state.gov/milestones/1945-1952/immigration-act.

6 Cherstin M. Lyon, "Alien Land Laws," Densho Encyclopedia, last updated October 8, 2020, https://encyclopedia.densho.org/Alien_land_laws.

7   "Luce-Celler Act of 1946," Immigration History: A Project of the Immigration and Ethnic History Society, Department of History, University of Texas at Austin, accessed August 3, 2023, https://immigrationhistory.org/item/luce-celler-act/.

8   "Truman's Veto," Maureen and Mike Mansfield Memorial Library, University of Montana, accessed August 3, 2023, http://exhibits.lib.umt.edu/omeka/exhibits/show/immigrant-montana/james-murray-and-immigration/truman-s-veto.

9   The complete story of Min Yasui and his remarkable family may be read in Lauren Kessler's book *Stubborn Twig* (Corvallis: Oregon State University Press, 2008).

10   Kessler, *Stubborn Twig*, 91-92.

11   Various sources quote a total of 110,000, others 120,000; Densho Encyclopedia explains that the first figure is the approximate number of people removed from their homes in the spring of 1942 under Executive Order 9066, and the larger number is roughly the total that passed through the camps throughout the war. Brian Niiya, "Ask a Historian: How Many Japanese Americans Were Incarcerated During WWII?," Densho Encyclopedia, June 2, 2021, https://densho.org/catalyst/how-many-japanese-americans-were-incarcerated-during-wwii/.

12   "Executive Order 9066: Resulting in Japanese-American Incarceration (1942)," United States National Archives and Records Administration, last reviewed January 24, 2022, https://www.archives.gov/milestone-documents/executive-order-9066.

13   Alan Rosenfeld, "German and Italian Detainees," Densho Encyclopedia, last updated July 29, 2015, https://encyclopedia.densho.org/German_and_Italian_detainees/.

14   "Honouliuli National Historic Site," National Park Service, US Department of the Interior, last updated January 4, 2017, https://www.nps.gov/hono/learn/historyculture/index.htm.

15   "Japanese Detention at Hawai'i Volcanoes," Hawai'i Volcanoes National Park, National Park Service, US Department of the Interior, last updated June 23, 2022, https://www.nps.gov/havo/learn/history-culture/japanese-detention.htm.

16   Densho Encyclopedia content director Brian Niiya states that taking into account all the camp residents, camp prisoners locked up by the FBI before and separate from the much bigger camps, and about 1,100 residents of Hawaii who were arrested, a total of 126,000 Japanese immigrants and Japanese Americans were imprisoned during World War

II, but I will stick with the 120,000 figure. Niiya, "Ask a Historian."

17 Daniel Immerwahr, *How to Hide an Empire: A History of the Greater United States* (New York: Farrar, Straus and Giroux, 2019), 175.

18 "President Gerald R. Ford's Proclamation 4417, Confirming the Termination of the Executive Order Authorizing Japanese-American Internment During World War II," February 19, 1976, Gerald R. Ford Presidential Library and Museum, https://www.fordlibrarymuseum. gov/library/speeches/.

19 Gary Y. Okihiro, "Department of Justice Camps," accessed August 3, 2023, https://reference.jrank.org/japanese/Department_of_Justice_ Camps.html.

20 "Terminology: Incarceration vs. Internment," Densho Encyclopedia, accessed August 3, 2023, https://densho.org/ terminology/#incarceration.

21 *Webster's New World College Dictionary*, 5th ed. (2014), s.v. "concentration camp."

22 *Oxford English Dictionary* (2023), "concentration camp."

23 · Lauren Kessler, *Stubborn Twig*, 97.

CHAPTER 8

1 Barbara Takei, "Tule Lake," Densho Encyclopedia, last updated October 16, 2020, https://encyclopedia.densho.org/Tule%20Lake/.

2 "Tule Lake Segregation Center," National Park Service, US Department of the Interior, accessed August 3, 2023, http://npshistory. com/brochures/tule/segregation-center.pdf.

3 "Tule Lake," Tule Lake National Monument, National Park Service, US Department of the Interior, last updated August 14, 2022, https:// www.nps.gov/places/tule-lake.htm.

4 Brian Niiya, "Civilian Exclusion Orders," Densho Encyclopedia, last updated June 12, 2020, https://encyclopedia.densho.org/Civilian%20 exclusion%20orders.

5 "Camp Layout," Tule Lake National Monument, US National Park Service, September 16, 2021, https://www.nps.gov/tule/planyourvisit/ camp-layout-pamphlet.htm.

6 Japanese American Veterans Association, "Over 800 Immigrant Japanese and Nisei Served in U.S. Army during World War I. Road to Gain Citizenship Was Long and Arduous," Discover Nikkei, June 3, 2019, https://discovernikkei.org/en/journal/2019/6/3/ wwi-veterans/; see also discussion of *Thind v. United States* (1923) at Immigration History: A Project of the Immigration and Ethnic

History Society, Department of History, University of Texas at Austin, accessed August 3, 2023, https://immigrationhistory.org/item/thind-v-united-states%E2%80%8B/.

7   Greg Robinson, *A Tragedy of Democracy: Japanese Confinement in North America* (New York: Columbia University Press, 2009), 308.

8   Takei, "Tule Lake."

9   "Tule Lake Segregation Center."

10 Edward Miyakawa, *Tule Lake* (House by the Sea, 1979).

11 United States v. Masaaki Kuwabara, 56 F. Supp. 716 (N.D. Cal. 1944), Justia US Law, accessed August 3, 2023, https://law.justia.com/cases/federal/district-courts/FSupp/56/716/1441113/.

12 Brian Niiya and Greg Robinson, "Wayne M. Collins," Densho Encyclopedia, last updated October 16, 2020, https://encyclopedia.densho.org/Wayne_M._Collins/.

13 Leverett Richards, "Repentant, Grieving Community Pays Debt of Honor in Funeral Services for Japanese-American War Hero," *The Oregonian*, September 12, 1948, 25.

CHAPTER 9

1   Tule Lake Center, "Final Reconciliation of All Train Lists," family collection.

2   "Life in the Camp," Heart Mountain WWII Japanese American Confinement Site, Heart Mountain Wyoming Foundation, accessed August 4, 2023, https://www.heartmountain.org/history/life-in-the-camp/.

3   "Heart Mountain Relocation Center," National Park Service, US Department of the Interior, last updated May 29, 2018, https://www.nps.gov/places/heart-mountain-relocation-center.htm.

4   Kara M. Miyagishima, *National Landmark Designation* (Washington, DC: National Park Service, November 2004), 21-22; cited in Mieko Matsumoto, "Heart Mountain," Densho Encyclopedia, last updated November 18, 2020, https://encyclopedia.densho.org/Heart%20 Mountain/.

5   Mike Mackey, *Heart Mountain: Life in Wyoming's Concentration Camp* (Powell, WY: Western History Publications, 2000), 38-40; cited in Matsumoto, "Heart Mountain."

6   US Department of the Interior, War Relocation Authority, Heart Mountain Relocation Center, "Name by Name Accounting of All Residents" for period ending December 31, 1944.

7   Ray Locker, "Heart Mountain Pilgrimage Features Tom Brokaw, Judge

Ito," *The Rafu Shimpo*, August 9, 2019, https://rafu.com/2019/08/heart-mountain-pilgrimage-features-tom-brokaw-judge-ito/.

8   Brian Niiya, "Ben Kuroki," Densho Encyclopedia, last updated July 19, 2022, http://encyclopedia.densho.org/Ben_Kuroki/.

9   Niiya, "Ben Kuroki," Interview Segment 11 (1998).

10 "Life in the Camp."

11 Meiko Matsumoto, "Heart Mountain," Densho Encyclopedia, last updated November 18, 2020, https://encyclopedia.densho.org/Heart%20Mountain.

12 Eric L. Muller, "Heart Mountain Fair Play Committee," Densho Encyclopedia, last updated July 2, 2020, https://encyclopedia.densho.org/Heart_Mountain_Fair_Play_Committee/.

13 "Life in the Camp."

14 "Heart Mountain Relocation Center."

15 "Heart Mountain Relocation Center."

16 "Joe Hayashi—Electronic Army Serial Number Merged File," US National Archives and Records Administration, accessed August 4, 2023, https://aad.archives.gov/aad/record-detail.jsp?dt=893&mtch=1&tf=F&q=joe+hayashi&bc=&rpp=10&pg=1&rid=7736521.

17 For accounts of Hayashi's and Okubo's actions that merited the award, see the Congressional Medal of Honor website, accessed August 4, 2023, https://www.cmohs.org/recipients/joe-hayashi and https://www.cmohs.org/recipients/james-k-okubo.

18 "Life in the Camp."

CHAPTER 10

1   "Facts and Case Summary—Korematsu v. U.S.," Administrative Office of the U.S. Courts, accessed August 6, 2023, https://www.uscourts.gov/educational-resources/educational-activities/facts-and-case-summary-korematsu-v-us.

2   "Korematsu v. United States, 323 U.S. 214 (1944)," Justia US Law, accessed August 6, 2023, https://supreme.justia.com/cases/federal/us/323/214/.

3   "Ex parte Endo, 323 U.S. 283 (1944)," Justia US Law, accessed August 6, 2023, https://supreme.justia.com/cases/federal/us/323/283/.

4   Greg Robinson, *By Order of the President: FDR and the Internment of Japanese Americans* (Cambridge, MA: Harvard University Press, 2001), 230.

5   Greg Robinson, *A Tragedy of Democracy: Japanese Confinement in*

North America (New York: Columbia University Press, 2009), 2.

6   Linda Tamura, *The Hood River Issei: An Oral History of Japanese Settlers in Oregon's Hood River Valley* (Urbana: University of Illinois Press, 1993), 216; cited in Linda Tamura, *Nisei Soldiers Break Their Silence* (Seattle: University of Washington Press, 2012), 139.

7   Lauren Kessler, *Stubborn Twig* (Corvallis: Oregon State University Press, 2008), 215.

8   "Nisei Return to Hood River," *Oregonian*, January 13, 1945, 1.

9   Linda Tamura, "Sherman Burgoyne," Densho Encyclopedia, last updated January 12, 2018, https://encyclopedia.densho.org/Sherman_Burgoyne/.

10 Kessler, *Stubborn Twig*, 214-15.

11 Wallace Turner, "Hatred of 1940's Still Vivid to Japanese," *New York Times*, July 20, 1981.

12 "Post to Consider Japs," *Oregonian*, October 23, 1919, 14.

13 Tamura, "Sherman Burgoyne."

14 US Department of the Interior, War Relocation Authority, Heart Mountain Relocation Center, "Name by Name Accounting of All Residents" for period ending December 31, 1944.

15 "Legion to Tell Stand Monday," *Oregonian*, December 4, 1944, 1.

16 Tamura, *Nisei Soldiers Break Their Silence*, 143.

17 "Churches Rap Legion's Act," *Oregonian*, December 2, 1944, 1.

18 "'Dual Citizenship' Target of Hood River Legion," *Oregonian*, December 5, 1944, 1.

19 "Nisei Invited by Legion Post," *Oregonian*, December 14, 1944, 1.

20 "War Secretary and Other Legionnaires Condemn Blacklisting of Loyal Nisei," *Oregonian*, December 15, 1944, 1.

21 "Hood River Jap Wounded," *Oregonian*, December 16, 1944, 4.

22 "Hood River Stand Told," *Oregonian*, December 20, 1944, 1; see also "'Dual Citizenship' Target," 1.

23 Tamura, *Nisei Soldiers Break Their Silence*, 142-43.

24 Tamura, "Sherman Burgoyne."

25 "Names of Vets Stay Off Roll," *Oregonian*, February 6, 1945, 1.

26 Tamura, *Nisei Soldiers Break Their Silence*, 151.

27 "Pro and Con of Current Events" (letters), *Oregonian*, December 24, 1944, 18.

28 "'No Comment,' on Japanese," *Oregonian*, December 19, 1944, 1.

29 Tamura, *Nisei Soldiers Break Their Silence*, 144, 148.

30 Tamura, *Nisei Soldiers Break Their Silence*, 147.

31 Tamura, *Nisei Soldiers Break Their Silence*, 137.

32 Tamura, *Nisei Soldiers Break Their Silence*, 146.

33 Tamura, *Nisei Soldiers Break Their Silence*, 154.

34 Richard L. Neuberger, "All Quiet on Hood River as Japs Return to Valley," *Sunday Oregonian*, June 16, 1946.

35 Daniel A. Poling, "Americans All," *Oregonian*, October 18, 1945, 11.

36 Tamura, *Nisei Soldiers Break Their Silence*, 164-65.

37 Lane Ryo Hirabayashi, "Hikaru Iwasaki," Densho Encyclopedia, last updated September 26, 2017, https://encyclopedia.densho.org/Hikaru_Iwasaki/.

38 Masuo Yasui, "Letter from Masuo Yasui to Sagoro Asai, 1946 January 18," Coll 956, Folder 2, Oregon Historical Society Research Library, accessed August 1, 2023, https://digitalcollections.ohs.org/coll-956-masuo-yasui-letter-to-sagoro-asai-1946-january-18.

39 Kessler, *Stubborn Twig*, 227.

40 Kessler, *Stubborn Twig*, 228-30.

41 Neuberger, "All Quiet on Hood River."

42 Richard L. Neuberger, "Their Brothers' Keepers," *Saturday Review of Literature*, August 10, 1946, 5-6, 27-28.

43 Quinn Stoddard, "Fariborz Maseeh Hall, Formerly Known as Neuberger Hall, Officially Opens Oct. 2," *PSU Vanguard*, September 30, 2019, https://psuvanguard.com/fariborz-maseeh-hall-formerly-known-as-neuberger-hall-officially-opens-oct-2/.

44 Adams Knight, "Richard and Maurine Neuberger Center," Portland State University, accessed August 6, 2023, https://www.pdx.edu/buildings/campus-building/richard-and-maurine-neuberger-center.

45 Tamura, "Sherman Burgoyne."

46 Tamura, "Sherman Burgoyne."

47 Email from Bo Bryan of the United Methodist Church, December 12, 2019.

48 "Asai-Namba," *Oregonian*, August 30, 1950, 17.

49 "Newlyweds to Live Here," *Oregonian*, March 7, 1954, 4.

50 Greg Robinson, "Japanese American Evacuation Claims Act," Densho Encyclopedia, last updated October 5, 2020, https://encyclopedia.densho.org/Japanese_American_Evacuation_Claims_Act/.

CHAPTER II

1 Ruth Adams Knight, "Girl without a Country?," *American Girl* 32, no. 8 (August 1949), 5-7, 40-42.

2 "Penny for Your Thoughts" [letters page], *American Girl* 32, no. 11 (November 1949, 30.

CHAPTER 12

1   "Awards Cap Junior Week," *Oregonian*, May 12, 1953.

EPILOGUE

1   Don Cogger, "A Journey Back to Heart Mountain," *Powell Tribune*, August 1, 2019, https://www.powelltribune.com/stories/a-journey-back-to-heart-mountain,20319.

2   "Original Root Cellar," Heart Mountain WWII Japanese American Confinement Site, Heart Mountain Wyoming Foundation, accessed September 3, 2023, https://www.heartmountain.org/donate-to-the-root-cellar-fund/.

3   "Oregon Legion Post Uses Veterans Day to Apologize for Past Mistakes," American Legion, November 17, 2022, at https://www.legion.org/honor/257515/oregon-legion-post-uses-veterans-day-apologize-past-mistakes.

About the Authors

Born on a fruit orchard in Hood River, Oregon, in 1932, MITZI ASAI LOFTUS spent three years of her childhood in government incarceration camps in California and Wyoming. For more than seventy years, she has given public talks about her family's experience to audiences of all ages. Having lived much of her adult life in Eugene and Coos Bay, she now resides in Ashland.

DAVID LOFTUS is the eldest of Mitzi's three sons, and a writer and editor in Portland, Oregon. He also does video and stage acting and voice work.